Putting Knowledge to Work

An American View of Ranganathan's Five Laws of Library Science

Pauline A. Atherton
Formerly Professor,
School of Library Science,
Syracuse University,
Syracuse, New York

Ess Ess Publications

4837/24, Ansari Road, Darya Ganj,
New Delhi-110002
✆ : 23260807, 51563444
Fax : 011-51563334
E-mail: info@essessreference.com
url:http://www.essessreference.com

Reprinted 1989
Reprint **2006**

ISBN: 81-7000-475-6

2;a1N:g
N73

Rs.250/-

Published By:
Ess Ess Publications
4837/24, Ansari Road,
Darya Ganj,
New Delhi-110 002
Ph.No. 23260807, 51563444, Fax: 51563334
E-mail: info@essessreference.com
url: www.essessreference.com
For:
Sarada Ranganathan Endowment for Library Science
702, 'Upstairs',
42nd Cross, III Block,
Rajajinagar,
Bangalore-560 010.
Ph.No. 23305109
E-mail: srels@vsnl.com

Printed in India at: Printline, New Delhi

CONTENTS

RANGANATHAN'S FIVE LAWS OF LIBRARY SCIENCE

1 Books are for use
2 Every Reader his/her book
3 Every book its reader
4 Save the time of the reader
5 A library is a growing organism

Learning from one's teacher constitutes a fourth part of knowledge. Another fourth part comes from associating with one's fellow students. The rest comes by his imparting the subject to his own pupils, or by expounding it in a public assembly.

—NAN NUL

The Good Book, A Thirteenth Century
Classic of Tamil Nadu, South India

CHAPTER A

PREFACE TO THE SERIES

The SARADA RANGANATHAN ENDOWMENT FOR LIBRARY SCIENCE was founded in 1963 by Dr S R Ranganathan and Mrs Sarada Ranganathan. Its funds are vested in the Treasurer of Charitable Endowments for India in accordance with Sections 4 and 5 of the Charitable Endowments Act, 1890 (6 of 1890). The Endowment is administered by a self-perpetuating Committee of five.

The objects of the Endowment are:

1 Furthering the cause of library science;

2 Organising periodically a course of lectures based on the latest ideas and research on library science and called, the SARADA RANGANATHAN LECTURES IN LIBRARY SCIENCE; and

3 Assisting in the publication of these lectures and of nascent ideas in library science.

The lectures can be delivered under the auspices of any university or any library association or any other body having similar interest and the funds can be spent in any part of India.

In fulfilment of the third objective, this series of books called Sarada Ranganathan Lectures is being published. They are based on the courses of lectures delivered by the respective authors at the invitation of the Endowment.

It is hoped that the books in this series will be of help in advancing library science and in improving library service.

Sarada Ranganathan Lectures

1;1965: From Little Acorns by B I Palmer

2;1966: United Nations Family of Libraries by P K Garde

3;1967: Sociological Foundations of Librarianship by J H Shera

4;1968: Development of the Theory of Library Classification by R S Parkhi

6;1970: Putting Knowledge to Work: An American View of Ranganathan's Five Laws of Library Science by Pauline Atherton

IN PREPARATION

5;1969; Teaching of Library Classification by D W Langridge

7;1971: Reference Service: The Penultimate Purpose of Library Work by Suseela Kumar

SPEECHES AT THE INAUGURAL FUNCTION

CHAPTER B

WELCOME ADDRESS

A Neelameghan, *Professor and Head, Documentation Research and Training Centre, Bangalore 560003, and Secretary, Sarada Ranganathan Endowment for Library Science.*

1 Introduction

On behalf of the Trustees of the Sarada Ranganathan Endowment for Library Science, I extend to you all a warm welcome, to this inaugural function and first lecture of the Sixth Series of the Sarada Ranganathan Lectures in Library Science. This evening, we are privileged to have two distinguished personalities on the dais — Shri K Guru Dutt, President of this evening's function, and Prof Pauline Atherton, the Sarada Ranganathan Lecturer for 1970.

2 K Guru Dutt

Shri Guru Dutt needs no introduction to the learned world of Bangalore. We all know him as a distinguished citizen and a scholar. There is hardly any cultural or learned body in Bangalore with which he is not connected in some way or other. And wherever he is, he adds grace to the occasion.

21 Bright Career

After a bright academic career, Shri Guru Dutt graduated in Mathematics from the Central College, Bangalore, in 1918. In his professional career, he started as a teacher in the Baldwin Girls' School, and then joined the Mysore Civil Service. He held successfully many different positions — such as, Assistant Commissioner in several of the districts of the Mysore State, City Magistrate, Secretary to the Mysore Constitutional Reforms Committee, Deputy Commissioner, Secretary on the Staff of the Maharaja of Mysore, Director of Food Supplies, and retiring as Director of Public Instruction in 1952 after being taken into the Indian Administrative Services retrospectively. He was also the first Chairman of the Mysore State Electricity Board from 1957 to 1960.

22 Academic Interests

Shri Guru Dutt loves books. He is a voracious reader and could speak with knowledge, spiced with humour, on almost any subject you can think of. His interests and scholarship are wide-ranging. He has been the Secretary of the Public Library of Bangalore for over six years, President of the

Mythic Society, and President of the Mysore Sanskrit Academy and similar learned bodies for several years. He has written a large number of articles and reviews to a variety of periodicals and newspapers. He has to his credit several books, such as *Hindu culture*; *Existentialism and Indian thought*; and *Pratibha*.

It was so kind and gracious of you, Sir, to have responded to our invitation to inaugurate the Sixth Sarada Ranganathan Lectures.

3 Prof Pauline Atherton

31 Friend of India

Prof Atherton was introduced to most of you this morning when she inaugurated the Eighth DRTC Seminar. Prof Atherton came to be known to Indian librarians as early as 1960 through her scholarly review of Dr Ranganathan's *Classified catalogue code* in the American periodical *Library resources and technical services*, and through her contribution to the first DRTC Seminar (1963). Since then she has generally been keeping up with the important contributions to library science from India, and making serious attempts to disseminate and interpret these ideas in the United States. Now that she is the President of the American Society for Information Science, she hopes to hold a balance between gadgetry on the one hand and the intellectual and social aspects of library science and service on the other.

32 Specialist Library Interests

Prof Atherton majored in the Social Sciences and took the M L S from the Rosary College in 1954. Her post-Masters Degree work in Library Science was done in the University of Chicago from 1955–61. Beginning in 1951, for over 15 years now, she has been working in specialist libraries and documentation centres of one kind or other. First, the Chemical Research Division of Corn Products Company from 1951–53, then the Art Department of the Chicago Public Library, followed by the Reference Department of the Chicago Teachers' College Library, from 1955–59. Documentalists are familiar with her work as the Director, Documentation Research Project of the American Institute of Physics, from 1961–66. Over the past decade, she has been a consultant to various specialist libraries, the *World book encyclopedia*, and research centres.

On the teaching side, she has been Associate Professor in the Chicago Teachers' College (1957–61), and Associate Professor, Syracuse University, since 1966. Currently she is a Visiting Professor in several

American universities. Prof Atherton's research interests include Mechanised Information Systems, the U D C, abstracting and indexing services, and computer-based laboratory facilities for education in library science.

33 On Professional Bodies

Among the many important positions she holds in professional organisations, mention may be made of her Vice-chairmanship of F I D/C R, A L A Committee on Accreditation, Sub-Committee to Revise Standards for Graduate Library Education, and the Advisory Council to U S Committee on Education for Library Research and Training.

34 Widely Travelled

Prof Atherton has travelled widely in U S A and in Europe to participate in seminars and conferences and to deliver lectures. She has to her credit several important papers and technical reports in the field of library science and documentation. The excellent editorial work she did on the proceedings of the Elsinore Conference is well known to documentalists.

I say it again that we are privileged to have such a distinguished personality as the Sarada Ranganathan Lecturer for 1970. A hearty welcome to you,

Madam, and we appreciate your gracious acceptance of our invitation to deliver this year's lectures.

4 Sarada Ranganathan Endowment for Library Science

The Sarada Ranganathan Endowment for Library Science, which sponsors these lectures, was founded by Dr Ranganathan and his family and was incorporated with the Treasurer of Charitable Endowments for India in 1963. Dr Ranganathan has turned into the funds of the Endowment the royalty accruing on his books, besides various donations he makes from time to time. Small donations are also received from other sources, such as the students and admirers of Dr Ranganathan and his works. The objectives of the Endowment are:

1 To further the cause of library science;

2 To organise periodically a course of lectures based on the latest ideas and research in library science and called the Sarada Ranganathan Lectures in Library Science; and

3 To assist in the publication of these lectures and of nascent ideas in library science.

The funds of the Endowment now stand at about Rs 2 lakhs. When it grows to a satisfactory level, we hope to have a chair or readership in library science established. In 1969, the Endowment gifted some 175 copies of Dr Ranganathan's *CC* and *CCC* to students in library schools in sixteen Indian universities. Award of scholarships for research in library science is also envisaged.

Since 1964 the Endowment has been publishing, in collaboration with the Documentation Research and Training Centre, the quarterly *Library science with a slant to documentation.*

5 Conclusion

Let me again extend to you all a hearty welcome. I now request Shri Guru Dutt, the President, to conduct the proceedings of this evening.

Thank you.

CHAPTER C

INAUGURAL ADDRESS
A LAYMAN'S REFLECTIONS ON LIBRARY SCIENCE

K Guru Dutt, *Director of Public Instruction (Retired), Mysore.*

1 Introduction

In the past, these lectures used to be inaugurated each time by a V I P. This year, I suppose by way of a change, a V U P has been asked to do so. I know I owe this invitation to the affection and generosity of Dr S R Ranganathan, and to the partiality of my friends in the DRTC, rather than to any merits of my own. Let me at the outset express my gratitude to them, and assure them how greatly I appreciate the honour. It is undoubtedly my *Adrishta*, a piece of good luck for me; but for you I am afraid it may be your *Prarabdha* or fate. If I fail to come up to the expectations, I would submit, the blame is not all mine.

2 Topic of the Address

On an occasion like this, I suppose I have to say a few words on some topic relevant to your major interests. Casting about for a theme, I decided on the title "A Layman's Reflections on Library Science." But it would be truer to say that my reflections are not so much on the contents of the science, as on the human predicament today as reflected in the outlook laymen associate with Library Science. Forgive me if I am frank at times, a bit too frank. You may interpret the word "reflections" in any sense you please.

3 Library Science

I am aware that almost overnight, Library Science has sprung forth fully armed like Minerva from the forehead of Jove. It has developed into a highly technical subject with a formidable literature of its own, which, let me confess, is *terra incognita* to me. Then why rush in where angels might fear to tread? My excuse is that a stranger touring a country may perchance notice things which the native misses. Possibly I may be able to view things from an unfamiliar angle, and say things not looked for.

4 Dangers of Extreme Specialisation

Let me start with a general observation. That extreme specialisation is the price to be paid for the advancement of science is a commonplace. But such specialisation necessarily narrows the vision and obstructs larger perspectives. So an expert has been facetitiously defined as one who comes to know more and more about less and less, until in the limit, he knows everything about nothing! Ortega y Gassett has gone to the length of dubbing a specialist as "a trained barbarian." Although Library Science also entails specialisation, yet its distinction is that the more you progress, the more general becomes your range and perspective. A true librarian is, or ought to be, primarily a purveyor of perspectives. But his knowledge has inevitably a skeletal and diagrammatic quality. It is mainly a knowledge of sign-posts and name-boards rather than of the country itself. The iron law of nature is that nothing can be had without paying its due price, although the day of reckoning may be postponed or forgotten. Your knowledge in its devotion to form runs the risk of loss of substance, to use the Aristotelian categories.

5 Ranganathan's Five Laws

I looked for inspiration to Dr Ranganathan's Five Laws of Library Science, which constitute, as it were, its *Panchasheela*. Their boldness and clarity is striking. They remind me of our ancient *Sutras*; but like them, they invite comment, and can stand a variety of interpretations. There is scope for a *prima facie* view (Purvapaksha), for doubts (Samsaya), and for arguments (*Samadhana*) leading up to conclusions (*Siddhanta*) which are perhaps immanent in the unspoken assumptions on which the line of reasoning is based. I am here venturing on an unorthodox, but brief commentary.

51 Law: 1: Books are For use

But in the orthodox way, I will first look at the commencement (*Upakrama*) and then at the close (*Upasamhara*) and enclose the other three laws within these limits. According to the first law, books are meant for use. Most certainly. Surely here at least there could be no room for difference of opinion. But the very next moment doubts raise their ugly head. What exactly do we mean by books? Surely not a mere collection of printed pages held together between covers, hard or paperback, irrespective of the nature and quality of their contents.

511 *Significance of the Term 'Use'*

Can we be certain that they will all be of use? What does "use" signify? It may mean different things in different contexts. I once knew a student who used Webster's big dictionary to supplement the height of his pillow; was he not using it? Commonly "use" suggests something basely utilitarian, a word which has a deprecatory and apologetic sound. It makes me uncomfortable, as marking something secondary, a servile means to some ulterior end. It is the goal or end which really interests us. Here, I recall the distinction drawn by John Dewey between instrumental and consummatory uses. It looks as if the modern world, in confusing the two, is more concerned with the means than with ends: means leading to further means and so on *ad infinitum,* without pausing to think of the significance of human existence—*Purushartha*—as we call it. The consequence of this headlong quest of means is the overlooking of meaning. That is our main trouble. Life has become a meaningless scramble. The revolt of youth, which is in evidence all the world over, has at its base this question: To what end is all this elaborate paraphernalia of a machine civilisation?

It is my deep-seated conviction that science has only instrumental value, except perhaps for its few genuine practitioners. My fear is that Library Science, as envisaged now, is mainly serving as the handmaiden of Science and Technology spelt with capitals. It seems to be pre-occupied with providing grist and facilities to the Information Industry. I do not wish to underestimate this need. But can that be the be-all and end-all of living?

Struggling for and with the amenities of life, we are forgetting to live. A lover of books all my life, still I honestly feel that the bulk of books are among the amenities which we could well spare without loss. Even the better type of books can easily become a distraction and even a vice. We could certainly do with fewer books from the standpoint of a happy life. But who cares for happiness in these days? It is excitement that we seek, and "divine discontent" that we worship.

6 Law 5: Library is a Growing Organism

I have done with the first law (*Upakrama*). Let us go to the last (*Upasamhara*). A library is a growing organism. I am afraid so. I have a sneaking sympathy with the outlook of the redoubtable Khalif Omar who said of the Koran: "Burn the libraries, for their value is in this book!"; and he straightaway proceeded to destroy the great library of Alexandria.

The point is that all growth is not necessarily good; it may be malignant and cancerous. Or from another standpoint, a virulent form of Parkinson's Law seems to dominate the world of books; and the mathematics of the situation makes me despair of Library Science being ever able to keep up with the tempo of growth. You will retort that that is no ground for giving up. I heartily agree and say "Cheerio!"

61 Proliferation of Ideas

You will permit me to digress a little. The Fourth Gospel commences with the glorious lines: "In the beginning was the Word, and the Word was with God." Since then, words have proliferated beyond measure and beyond all control. The result of this inflation has been catastrophic devaluation of the Word (Logos) itself. It is a lost concept, a loss which nothing can make good. Can it be a measure of our progress from the beginning, that we are already nearing the end of the world?

Of late, we are hearing a great deal about the world crisis brewing due to the fast pollution of the environment: the geosphere, the hydrosphere, and the atmosphere. But it appears to me that the root cause lies in neither of these tangible spheres, but solely in the pollution of the *noosphere* — to use a term coined by Teilhard de Chardin — the sphere of knowledge and ideas, in other words, of books.

No doubt, with the phenomenal growth of knowledge, this is inevitable to some extent. Yet we cannot ignore the destructive potentialities of knowledge. That is the significance of the Biblical legend of the forbidden fruit.

7 Maintaining a Balance

71 Principle of Yoga

Our own ancestors had always realised the need for a principle of control over the trend towards endless expansion, a doctrine of balance and limit if the ship of humanity is to be kept on an even keel. In uptodate terminology, a "negative feed-back" is essential if the "homeostasis" necessary for a healthy life is to be maintained. In India, such a principle formed the core of the discipline known as *Yoga*. It aimed at the elimination of distractions, especially in the shape of words, and the achievement of a creative silence. But in the world of today, we see on the contrary, the operation of a deadly sort of "positive feedback," a centrifugal force unchecked by a counterpart centripetal energy to keep us in orbit.

72 Absorb a Few Good Books

To return to our main topic, I remember that as a boy I was greatly impressed by an essay entitled *The man of one book* by Isaac Disraeli, father of the famus Benjamin Disraeli. The essay dilated on the benefits of character and expression accruing to a reader who stuck to one sole book. The practice has its points. The Bible and Shakespeare read in this way contributed to what is best in British life. Similarly, it is impossible to estimate how much

India owes to the *parayana* of the *Ramayana* or the *Mahabharata*. They comprehend the whole of our culture. As the latter claims proudly but not without justice: "In regard to the four-fold goal of human life, what is found here may be found elsewhere but what is not here is nowhere."

73 Speed is not Always Good

But what about ourselves? We seem to be more impatient than the princess in the Arabian Nights who demanded a new husband every night. We hanker for change, the more the better. We have no time to spare. That is what the fourth law suggests to me, when it adjures us to save the time of the reader and of the staff. The computer has become our model, and will perhaps displace man one day. Speed is our ideal and our principal bane. My doubt is: Save time for what? For, when we have saved the time, we do not know what to do with it, unless we reinvest it, like capital, to launch more enterprises to save more time. Such is our predicament.

So far as the reader is concerned, I feel that the value of a book is inversely proportional to the speed with which he tackles it. The right thing to do is, as in the case of the heart patient, to go slow. If the book is worthwhile, the reader would be well advised to go as slow as he can, tasting each word and sentiment and enjoying the whole.

But if it is not worthwhile, the sooner it is cast aside, the better. There are other ways of spending time. In any case, we should be more heedful that time be well spent, rather than merely saved.

8 Law 2 and Law 3

Finally I come to the twin laws: Every book its reader; and every reader his book. The democratic fervour breathing through these two laws leaves me speechless. Their implication (*Dhvani*) is that a book and its reader have each equal rights. But in reality, they are by no means on a par. I am old-fashioned enough to share Bacon's opinion that some books are to be tasted, others to be swallowed, and only a few to be chewed and digested. Bacon leaves out a large class which Dr Ranganathan includes: those which do not deserve to be read and should forthwith be liquidated. But who is to decide? Of course, the reader for himself, and the library expert for the library; although no such decision can pretend to be final.

81 Reader-Book Relationship

In truth, the relationship between a book and its reader is highly complex. Except in a purely physical sense, a book is no unit. As Pascal said three centuries ago, and thinkers like Ortega and Aldous Huxley in our time, thoughts are as it were atomic.

The common experience also confirms that ideas and words are the actually viable units. The *Vakyapadiya* of the great Bhartrihari, a fifth century treatise on the philosophy of language, is so named because it maintains that sentences and words are the basic quanta of communication. Their being strung together in a book (*grantha*) is adventitious. Books are indeed of very unequal texture. As Emerson has rightly said, "Even from Plato I can at best extract a dozen sentences of lasting value."

82 VALUE OF A BOOK

The notion of value is however a notorious variable depending on the reader's calibre and sensibilities, as well as on his temperament and even the passing mood. No reader is the same at all times, and his reaction to books, even to one and the same book, is changeable. Of course I am speaking of true books and not of compendia of information masquerading as books. The relation between a book and a reader is by no means constant; and it is no use trying to simplify it. For, as Whitehead has observed: "Every simplification is an over-simplification."

9 Conclusion

I have finished, and I can see you heaving a sigh of relief. Have I been controversial? Yes, deliber-

LECTURES BY
PAULINE ATHERTON

CHAPTER D

INTRODUCTION

1 Attracted by Dr Ranganathan's Work

It is indeed an honour for me to be here with Dr Ranganathan and his students in his home-land. I have introduced myself to many groups in the United States as an apostle of Ranganathan. Now I have the opportunity to tell a group in his own land why I have given myself such a title.

11 First Impression

More years ago than I care to remember, even at my age, I heard of Ranganathan. It was in a course on the History and Theory of Cataloguing at the University of Chicago, I had already received my Master's Degree in Library Science, and was working as a librarian. It was in this advanced course that I first learned of the "Father of library science in India." Let me recall for you what my first impressions were when I pursued the request that Mrs Ruth French Strout made of me in a seminar to find out something about Ranganathan's catalogue code and report back to the class. I remember them quite well because my immediate impression upon reading the five statements called "The Five Laws of Library Science" in the first book by Dr Ranganathan that I found, was one of amusement. Yes, I smiled, and thought to myself, "how simple he makes it all sound, when really it is much more complicated!"

2 Depth of the Five Laws

After that, I thought about these five short statements and decided that no more really needed to be said to force me to think seriously about the most important areas of library service, evaluation, and management. Ever since that day fifteen years ago, I have been guided by those words when I pursued advanced technological developments and applied them to library and information work, or when I would begin a class on the organisation of information, cataloguing, or library in society. I have written these five statements on every blackboard in every classroom where I have taught and I will continue to do so, because they offer me (and my students) the guidance and the rationale we need when we critically review how we follow the cataloguing practices which prevail, how we evaluate the libraries we use, visit, or work in, and how we work to improve the practices we follow and the library services we manage. Because these five statements have served as my guiding star throughout my professional library career, I would like to use them as the framework for my Sarada Ranganathan Lectures, being delivered at the Documentation Research and Training Centre which Dr Ranganathan helped to found.

3 An Opportunity to Review

I appreciate the invitation to deliver these lectures in Bangalore. This has served as my needed opportunity to pull together my thoughts on the topics which mean a great deal to me; namely, library education, library use, system evaluation, and improvements in the principles and practices of cataloguing and classification based on assistance from computers and empirical research. Because I am so deeply touched by this opportunity, I may tend to be overly personal in my remarks rather than purely scientific and scholarly. Hopefully, this will not detract from my presentation too much. I hope that my review of several studies on these topics recently completed by my colleagues in the United States (some of them former students) will add the substance needed to make these lectures as beneficial to the listener (or reader) as they are to the writer.

The information on the emergence of the Five Laws (*See* Chapter K) has been provided by Prof A Neelameghan.

CHAPTER E

LAW 1: BOOKS ARE FOR USE: HOW TO SEE TO IT!

1 Improvising the Usability of Documents

During the 1960's in the United States, a great many developments have taken place in trying to improve the usability of documents (all printed forms of messages and data, that is, recorded knowledge). More often than not, the headlines are made when a bigger or better computing system is used, but we should not confuse ourselves: the improvements came because a competent staff investigated the problems presently faced by users trying to get documents to use, investigated the user himself, and his channels of communication, and the media he selects to find information. Only when they were sure that he values the use of documents above other media have they tried to improve his access by the use of computers or other mechanical devices. Many studies and efforts could be cited and their findings quoted, but let one study of physicists serve as an example.

2 Media for Information and Communication

Twelve different media were cited by the physicists surveyed as best performing seven information functions:

*1 Articles in periodicals read in *own, or library copy*;

2 Reprints they collect;

*3 Manuscripts (including drafts) they receive from author;

4 Technical reports distributed within own institution;

5 Technical reports distributed by other than own institution;

6 Telephone conversation;

*7 Face-to-face discussions with persons working in their institution;

8 Face-to-face discussions with persons not currently working in their institution (e g, at scientific meeting, etc);

9 Oral presentations made at scientific meetings or conferences;

10 Copies of oral presentations (including lecture notes and conference proceedings);

11 Private correspondence; and

12 Other.

*Found to be most important.

3 Needs of Readers, or Information Dissemination Function

The following were considered to be the main objectives of use of the different media mentioned in Section 2.

1 General awareness of current state of physics;

2 Find out who is working in what area or on what problems;

3 Source of specific ideas for work *in progress;*

4 Source of specific ideas for *new* work;

5 Inform others of my research activities;

6 Getting up-to-date in a new area; and

7 Browsing stimulation.

The study showed the high value of articles in periodicals and manuscripts in respect of all the seven of the information functions. With this knowledge, the American Institute of Physics proceeded with their plans for a computer-based information system to publish and disseminate information in the field of Physics in printed form. Because face-to-face discussions with persons were the second most important media with respect to meeting the information needs (3) and (4) above, the American Institute of Physics expanded its responsibility for organising meetings for the members of its member societies. They have sought new and better ways of performing these important information dissemination functions because they recognise that "books are for use."

4 CICIN Conference

41 LIBRARY NETWORK

A recent conference in USA at Airlie, near Warrenton, Virginia, brought one hundred leaders in the American library and communications world together to discuss and make recommendations for national policy regarding library and information networks. Without the dedication that *books are for use,* it would have been difficult for some to agree to certain recommendations because they conflict with their institutional objectives. For the greater good, then, the group established certain goals for *library network services.* I cite them here to indicate how far Dr Ranganathan's first law can be pursued.

At the CICIN meeting sponsored by ALA, we agreed that *it is a legitimate need of every library or information centre to call upon information networks to identify, locate and make available all forms of materials and services and to provide efficient and dependable information delivery services to the ultimate seeker of information.* This implies a freer interinstitutional communication structure.

42 MAKING READERS AWARE OF INFORMATION

We agreed at the Airlie Conference that the major goal in the provision of information services through a library network should be to facilitate *learning* in its broadest sense. Libraries and other information centres at the present time are able to provide the storage, retrieval, and display systems for information that can be utilised by a *limited* number of patrons with a fairly well defined need and clearly articulated demand for services. Use of these services is conditioned by the perceived expectation of satisfaction on the part of the user. Success reinforces usage and disappointment leads the patron to seek elsewhere or to let his needs go unfulfilled. To have continued use of our libraries and information centres, initiative must be taken by the service agency to make their services known to potential users. They must develop the means and take a more active role in identifying and defining a patron's need for information. Let us call these *awareness* services — one of our first tasks.

43 BIBLIOGRAPHICAL SERVICE: MEDIATION

To use information for learning, the perceived

need for information must be translated into the provision of information to meet that need. This *mediation function* depends on the interpretation of the need, and on the availability and use of *directory systems* and *consulting services* that lead to the eventual delivery of the information and information services needed. Thus, the second function to be performed by a service network of libraries and information centres is the provision of information *about* information and information systems. We call this *bibliographic* or *intellectual* access.

44 Physical Access to Documents

In addition to this intellectual access, provision for physical access by *delivery* systems will make information available in the place, time, and form that is best suited to the user. It is recognised that the problems of resource management and control in a network will be exceedingly complex, but that these problems must be solved with a primary view towards the more expeditious delivery of informational media to meet service demands.

45 Evaluation of Service

Even with a network with objectives to provide awareness, mediatory access, and delivery service, we still agreed at the CICIN Conference that the network must provide an *evaluation* service both to aid the user in guiding his behaviour, and sensing his opinion. We need the necessary feedback mechanisms at all levels which will make such a network adaptive to changing patterns of need and use. In this sense, the network is itself a learning mechanism which is aware of both its parts and the environment in which it operates and is able to modify its behaviour accordingly.

5 Change of Pattern of Service

These five services — awareness, mediation, access, delivery, and evaluation — describe the user-system interface in terms of the benefits to be provided by an information network. This delineation of services at Airlie seems to be a natural extension of the First Law if we put it into a larger context of library and information networks. There should be no mistake that, what is being contemplated under the term library and information, something quite new and different from conventional library systems is envisioned. It is a new medium for the dissemination of knowledge. Are we librarians prepared for such a change in our professional lives?

Such developments as information networks, and system evaluation studies in the U S have brought about a general awareness that either books are for use or libraries should not be supported and stay in business. Many people have strongly criticised "traditional library service" in the United States and have questioned whether the established methods are the ones to perpetuate.

6 Impact on Library Education

Such reports as *Libraries at Large, Library Response to Social Change*, and the new A L A Policy on Education and Manpower force us in library education in the United States to engage in some self-evaluation and reassessment of our curriculum. We have to ask ourselves: how do we teach the new version of the First Law of Library Science? I am not sure library education in India is undergoing such upheaval, but reflections on developments in one country may quite possibly have some relevance for our colleagues elsewhere. The following remarks are offered in that spirit.

Students in American library schools are asking for a new curriculum and for class activities which are relevant to today's and tomorrow's libraries. Should we admit that library education goals need to be revamped? Can we stem the tide of increasing irrelevancy of many of our libraries today? One possibility I suggested in a talk I delivered in Texas in the Spring of 1970 was to "put knowledge to work" in today's library schools. Knowledge about librarianship, I contended, exists in the form of library research and development efforts which are available but not always integrated quickly into a library school curriculum. D W MacKinnon (8). said this about the word *knowledge*:

"Knowledge is the result of playing with what we know, that is, with our facts. *Ledge,* the second element in the word *knowledge,* means apart. A knowledgeable person in science is not, as we are often wont to think, merely one who has an accumulation of facts, but rather one who has the capacity to have sport with what he knows, giving creative rein to his fancy in changing his world of phenomenal appearances into a world of scientific constructs."

A knowledgeable person in librarianship, then, would be someone who has the facts as well as the experience of using these facts, taking them apart as a young boy might examine a clock. If the object of library science education would be to develop creative and knowledgeable librarians, then the stage must be set for this. Passive learners do not make creative librarians. Passing an examination or series of examinations is not the best criterion for judging professional promise, or certifying that someone is a knowledgeable person.

Instead of the usual array of admission tests, lectures, class work, term papers, reading lists, and oral reports, I ask you to imagine a library school which would operate as follows.

61 Admission to Library Course

The object of the *admission procedure* would be to determine if the student has the potential to develop in professional competence and take his full responsibility as a librarian. To ascertain this potential, he would be interviewed by "library school representatives" (professional librarians in the field near the student's home who know the library school's objectives). This new student would also be interviewed by faculty and students currently enrolled in the school. These interviews would be designed to determine the candidate's capacity for independent thinking, intelligence, and potential competence as a professional librarian.

62 Initial Orientation

As for curriculum content and method of presentation, the transmission of basic facts, skills and techniques would be by means of an independent study programme. Faculty would be on call for special classes or meetings on certain topics but would not have regular classes as such covering these basic skills. Some faculty might run laboratories where exercises in basic skills could be performed or they might operate experimental libraries as part of their teaching/research load. This activity might require anywhere from one to three months of the student's time, depending on his rate of development and on a consensus of what we consider to be *the* basic skills or knowledge.

63 Research on Specific Library Problems

After this initial orientation and basic learning period, the student would be placed in direct contact with various research problems associated with library developments. Either formal courses or directed field work would be arranged for this portion of his education. The faculty would approach this phase of library education as colleagues rather than as teachers of the students. The students would help choose the subject matter and possible projects which would have relevance for their own purposes and development. Real problems in libraries could form the basis for projects; sometimes the work would be brought to the school's laboratory and at other times, the *students* and *faculty* would study and work at the library in the field. Any problem deemed manageable could be pursued with the guidance of the faculty and the librarians in charge. In this way, the necessary theories and principles, methods and advanced knowledge could

more of class-discussions, tutorials, colloquia, seminars, and project work. The lectures are mainly for raising the curtain, as it were, to point to some areas of research in the field. That some of the students are able to turn out pieces of research in library science even while they are undergoing the course, is an indication of the effectiveness of the methods used.

It is also noteworthy that evaluation of student work and of the effectiveness of the programme is based on project work — individual and cooperative — in each of the subjects rather than on answering a two-hour or three-hour question paper.

7 The Challenge

71 Change of Programme Needed

Will faculty in library schools be willing to admit that a series of courses, no matter what their content, is not sufficient preparation for the responsibilities the student should assume upon graduating? It is difficult to see a working alternative if we are to implement in the United States the proposed A L A statement of the objective of the master's programmes in librarianship. The A L A statement says, "the objective . . . should be to prepare librarians capable of participating and engineering the change and improvement required to move the profession constantly forward." Concentrating on the tasks and routines in today's libraries will not do this nor will a purely academic library education. We need to relate the library school student to the library profession's present problems and future needs.

72 Two Phases of Library Education

If knowledge in librarianship is to be seriously pursued, we must find the capacity to have sport with what we know. No longer can we assume that knowledge in librarianship is merely the accumulation of brick-upon-brick of content and information — that is something to be taught in a basic set of courses or learned on the job. Instead, we should look at library education as a two phase operation; first we will have to master certain skills and facts, and secondly we will have to approach some of the problems of librarianship as researchers and scholars. Library schools should be where this happens, where fledgling librarians sprout their wings under the guidance of experienced professionals.

73 Change of Attitude Called For

If this approach sounds interesting to you, there is a crucial question for students, library educators and librarians alike: can we abandon some of the assumptions we now have about library education? Students quite often assume that courses and experiences in library school will be like their other classes; faculty expect to teach course by course and assume it is difficult to innovate; librarians would find it difficult to fit both library school faculty and students into their work-a-day world. Everyone will need to be re-oriented if we are to develop a programme whose graduates will be tomorrow's decision-makers in libraries. We will all have to work to find ways for the students to demonstrate that they are able to make original, significant contributions to professional practice.

74 Relate Library Education to Library Problems

Such a school, as I envision, would include direct experimental confrontation with research problems and other practical, ethical and philosophical problems. The students would relate their educational experiences to the real problems being faced today and those likely to come up in the near future. Before such a school could open its doors, several librarians would have to agree to have their libraries designated as "library education experimental stations"; library educators would have to accept their role as researchers and field workers;

and students would have to assume their role as colleagues working on more than studying library problems.

8 Library Education Experimental Project

81 A Personal Note

This past year, we tried to put part of this plan to work for such a library school at the Syracuse University. We established something called the LEEP Laboratory. Before I can begin to describe it, I would like to tell you some personal history to put it all into some context.

More than ten years stretch between my library school days as a student and my being a member of the faculty at Syracuse University School of Library Science. During much of that time, I was engaged in documentation research (later called information storage and retrieval systems) in the field of scientific information. Libraries and librarians were not the stars of the drama I witnessed during those years, although I thought we had a lot to contribute as well as a lot to learn from the whole endeavour. When I returned to library education and tried to relate some of the excitement I felt about the developments in information systems, I met the same looks and attitudes that you do when you show your slides of Europe to a group that has never been there. Gradually, I realised that what I had witnessed could only come alive if the audience was given first-hand experiences; if, in other words, they were able to play with their knowledge and have sport with what they knew. The problem was: How to bring information storage and retrieval concepts into a traditional library school with no strong resources or faculty in special librarianship or computers.

82 Providing Real Experience of Automation

The United States Office of Education and the Library of Congress came to my rescue with financial and technical resources to help us transform some of the class discussion of library automation and information storage and retrieval systems. We created LEEP, the Library Education Experimental Project. It is a laboratory environment where the students and faculty have experience with a computer-based catalogue, developed from the MARC Pilot Project data from the Library of Congress. We have learned to use the MARC records in the computer as a library user now uses the cards in a card catalogue. Students and faculty began to evaluate the bibliographic control system within a library by contrasting it with this new tool. Some students are taking the initiative and are engaged in independent projects where they work with a librarian in the field to study and suggest improvements in existing systems. The impact of MARC in libraries has been brought home to every student regardless of his orientation to school, public, academic, or special libraries because every student in the school experiences some use of MARC when he takes courses in cataloguing, reference service or bibliography. All of these courses have assignments of one kind or another which bring the student to the LEEP Laboratory.

83 A Cooperative Effort

LEEP had as consultants the two librarians in the Syracuse area most directly involved with advanced library automation projects — Ron Miller of the Five Associated University Libraries and Irwin Pizer of the Biomedical Communications Network. They advised us as we developed the LEEP Laboratory. Some of our students in turn contributed something to their research efforts. More than three hundred students at Syracuse during 1969-70 had at least a brush with the computer-based MARC catalogue. The students say they went away feeling less fearful about the "machine." Some of the faculty were glad that LEEP existed because they were able to demonstrate certain concepts and new developments instead of merely talking about them.

84 LEEP-BY-MAIL SERVICE

At an institute in the Adirondack Mountains in October 1969, faculty from twenty library schools came to see what we had done. At that time, we implemented a LEEP-by-Mail service. Now students in other library schools, where computing facilities and the MARC data base are not as accessible, can perform MARC searches in our LEEP laboratory and they too can put this knowledge to work, testing the potential of MARC, etc! As of this date, some fifty or more students in two library schools in New York and Philadelphia are using LEEP.

9 Faith in Collective Effort

I have great faith in the combined efforts of librarians, students and faculty in library schools today. Together we will find a way to insure that books are used and that this will be our first goal. The absolute essential for success will depend, of course, on our willingness to have sport with what we know. Librarianship is a practical world but it is on the edge of a new existence. If we look at ourselves in a playful way and use the knowledge we gain, we could make our education more relevant and our graduate librarians more professional. If we make an effort to establish a *quid pro quo* relationship between the field of library work and library education, we can insure the implementation of the First Law of Library Science.

Philip H Rhinelander said, "Education ought to be ultimately not a matter of systems, nor of organisations, or of structures, or of theories, but of individuals who *encounter* one another, who respect one another, who can speak to one another, despite disagreements, and who can *listen*" (18). Such an opportunity as this is my education, my encounter, and my chance to listen as well as speak.

CHAPTER F

LAW 2: EVERY READER HIS BOOK: HOW TO KNOW THE READER IN SEARCH OF HIS BOOK

> There are some things which cannot be learned quickly, and time, which is all we have, must be paid heavily for their acquiring.
>
> —Ernest Hemingway

1 Need for "Use Studies"

Most libraries appear committed to the doctrine of service to patrons, to facilitating the reader's search for his book. Oftentimes, however, doubts have arisen in our minds as to whether or not we are providing those facilities which, in fact, best meet the needs of patrons. Out of these doubts have come numerous "use studies" in the United States and elsewhere which contribute to our knowledge of the reader (or user) and sometimes provide us with the information needed to redesign our libraries to give better performance.

2 Catalogue Use Studies

The 1960's have seen a great many surveys of

use studies, accompanied with justifiable criticism of the research methodologies used and the unreliability of the findings. Two studies in the United States have recently been reported, which rise above these criticisms and serve as fine examples of how to investigate the following questions:

1 Who uses the library?

2 For what purpose is the card catalogue consulted?

3 With what success is the catalogue consulted?

4 How was the catalogue card utilised? Which items on the card were used? Do different classes of users make different use of the items on the catalogue card?

5 Would a hypothetical reduced catalogue meet the needs of most users of the card catalogue (that is, would a catalogue, consisting of author, title, subject headings, call number, and date of publication, suffice)?

Because this area of library research is so important, I would like to concentrate on these two studies of the user at the card catalogue, explaining the methodology used in some detail, the most interesting findings, and the implications of their work for improvement of library services in general.

Consider this information exchange with me serving as the catalyst, since neither Richard Palmer (10) nor Ben-Ami Lipetz (6) can be here to discuss their work first hand. I will leave behind, in India, however, their reports, with the compliments of the authors. They gave me permission to discuss their work in detail with you. For this, I am grateful.

21 Population Studied

The Palmer study consisted of the users of the University of Michigan General Library card catalogue. The sample, obtained by means of a two-stage probability sampling model, consisted of 5,067 users of the card catalogue who completed questionnaires during an eight-week survey during the Fall Term of 1967.

The Lipetz study was conducted in the Sterling Memorial Library of Yale University. The pattern of traffic flow in the catalogue area was determined by means of frequent traffic counts that were continued for more than a year. The observed traffic flow was used as the basis for designing the interview schedule that would encompass a thoroughly representative sample of catalogue users.

The Lipetz study at Yale went beyond catalogue use and traced the users' starting clues at the catalogue through to use of books and the front matter from these books and their representation on catalogue cards.

Palmer reviewed over eighteen card catalogue use studies and found all but five lacking in their definition of population studied. This is a basic concern in research design and the connection between knowledge of our population and our stated goals of service is very straightforward. One cannot create an ideal tool of any sort on a rational basis (whether that tool be a conventional catalogue, a computerised catalogue, or any other device for any other application) without knowing a good deal about the purpose or purposes for which the tool is to be used, and about the manner in which the users interact with the tool (11).

The careful way in which Palmer and Lipetz established the population for their user surveys deserves repeating.

3 Methodology

31 Population Studied: University of Michigan Library

Palmer chose the actual users of the University of Michigan General Library card catalogue as the survey population. In the process of establishing the population for the user survey at Michigan, he rejected as the survey population such possible populations as all individuals officially connected with the University of Michigan or all users of the University of Michigan General Library because it was not possible to establish from available data that the characteristic of these potential populations matched the population of the users of the card catalogue.

In order, however, to provide some background on the general environment in which the survey was conducted, it is noted that the study was conducted at the University of Michigan General Library card catalogue room during the Fall Term, 1967, at which time the student enrolment at the University of Michigan totalled 37,283. Of those enrolled, 21,087 were undergraduates, 9,729 were graduates, and 3,698 were graduate-professionals. Included in the 37,283 students were 2,769 who were enrolled in credit extension (mostly graduate). The faculty numbered more than 3,800; other academic staff, about 2,500; and non-academic staff, including part-time employees, totalled about 13,700. As indicated above, these categories of potential patrons were not selected as the survey population because the configuration of their use of the card catalogue could not be predicted from available data and because users other than those officially connected with the University of Michigan would be likely to use the card catalogue during the eight-week survey period.

During the survey period (September 11 to November 5, 1967), 186,768 persons passed through the turnstiles at the entrances to the University of Michigan General Library. Thus, an average of 23,346 persons per week patronised the General Library during tne eight weeks of the survey. These patrons were not, however, selected as the survey population because the configuration of their use of the card catalogue could not be predicted from available data.

It was therefore the decision of this study that actual users of the University of Michigan General Library card catalogue during the survey period would comprise the survey population. It was further decided that no attempt would be made to ascertain the exact number of such users. Rather, a team of students conducted a physical head count of patrons using the card catalogue during one week, February 20–26, 1967, during the 101 hours that the library was open. The count came to a total of 5,778 persons. On the basis of this count, it was estimated that approximately 48,000 persons would use the card catalogue during the survey period. This estimated number of persons constituted the survey population. The survey was then designed to sample not less than ten per cent of this estimated population, or not less than 4,800 patrons. It was determined that a ten per cent sample, clustered and systematically randomized, should provide findings of statistical reliability at the .05 level of significance, for which a reasonable confidence interval could be computed, and from which useful predictions regarding the total user population could be made.

32 Population Studied: Yale University

Lipetz chose a similar survey population (7), namely, the actual users of the card catalogue at the Yale University Library, but his technique for sampling this population involved a careful observation over a total of 62 weeks of the traffic flow at the card catalogue.

321 *Traffic Flow Management*

Lipetz thought that the determination of the pattern of people entering the catalogue area was a key factor in the later design of an interviewing schedule which would yield a clearly representative sample of catalogue users. The pattern of entry to the catalogue was determined by having observers assigned to count the number of people entering the catalogue area through different entryways during different times of day and days of the week. Observers were stationed where they could observe simultaneously either the front three aisles into the catalogue or the rear two aisles into the catalogue. For a period of five minutes' duration, they would count the number of persons entering each of the aisles being observed. Timing periods were rigidly predetermined to cover different hours of the day, different days of the week, and even different tenths of each hour. Observation assignments were rigidly scheduled; the schedule repeated every seven weeks. Observations were continued over a total of 62 weeks so as to provide a ten-week overlap period for determination of any annual variation in traffic which might occur. (During this 62-week period, there was a 5-week interruption in observations, during the late summer, while shifting of catalogue drawers was going on; the abnormal shifting activity tended to interfere with traffic flow).

The total amount of time during which traffic was counted was somewhat over 4 per cent of the time that the library was open during the total time span involved. For practical reasons, the coverage was more intense during weekday working hours (6 per cent) and lower during evening hours and weekends (about 2.5 per cent). However, observed traffic was also lower (by about one-fourth) during evening hours and weekends. Tallies of traffic counts by hour, day and entryway for the first ten weeks of observation were used as the basis for designing the interviewing schedule. Traffic counts were continued during the interviewing period to check on the continuing validity of the pattern observed during those first ten weeks and to provide a rational basis for weighting of interview results if the interview schedule should prove to be biased with respect to observed traffic.

Several other traffic measurements were made in addition to the counts of persons entering the catalogue area: At precise preassigned times, observers would follow anyone entering the catalogue to observe where he went (which catalogue drawer), how long he stayed at the catalogue, and how many call-number notations he wrote down. Intervals for conducting these observations were scheduled in exactly the same pattern as intervals for gross traffic counts so as to cover all times of catalogue availability.

Observers of catalogue traffic were instructed to avoid counting those library staff members who regularly work in the catalogue area (filers, verifiers, reference librarians). The intent of the measurements was to count, as far as possible, only the "consumers" of the catalogue service, rather than the suppliers and interpreters.

Methods for the collection of data differed in the two studies, but both appear to have been rigorous applications of the statistically reliable methods they chose to employ. They are explained here to illustrate how two different methods can be employed for achieving the same objective. The survey periods were at first approximately the same — eight weeks at Michigan and ten weeks at Yale, but Yale continued their interviewing over a full year. The questions asked and techniques used varied as the following excerpts from the two reports show.

33 Sampling: Michigan University Library

At Michigan, the population was defined as the users of the card catalogue during the survey period, September 11 to November 5, 1967 (12). The sample size was established as ten per cent of the population. A one-page questionnaire, including an illustrative catalogue card, with items on the card identified by means of red exponential numbers and a list of items on the catalogue card numbered in red placed immediately below the illustrative card, was selected as the survey instrument. Questionnaires were distributed to selected patrons as they entered the catalogue room and were collected as they left.

A two-stage probability sample using systematic selection was chosen for the survey. (*See* Sec 31).

The estimated figure of 48,000 patrons was based, as mentioned earlier, on a physical head count of users conducted during the week ending 26 February 1967. In this two-stage probability sample, the frame of the sample was taken to be all users of the General Library card catalogue during the eight-week period, September 11 to November 5, 1967. The hours of the week in which the library was open were the first-stage sample units, and the users in each of the selected hours were the second-stage sample units. The outline of the sample design is as follows:

1 Measures of size were assigned to hours (clusters) according to the probable number of users in each of them. As it was expected that there would be some random fluctuation in the number of users, the measures of size were corrected to the nearest unit of twenty to simplify the operation.

2 Under-sized clusters (hours when few users were expected) were linked or combined to insure that each selected cluster would yield a reasonable number of users.

3 The method of selection used was probability proportional to size in the first-stage and probability inversely proportional to size in the second stage in order to give an overall equal probability of selection to each user.

4 Systematic selection was employed in both the first-stage and second-stage selections.

331 *Questionnaire*

A survey team composed of eleven students enrolled in the Department of Library Science conducted the survey. During systematically selected hours, questionnaires were handed to a random sample of about twenty patrons as they entered the catalogue room, were completed by the patrons while in the catalogue room, and were collected by the survey team as the patrons left. The survey team was available throughout the 240 survey hours to answer any questions that the patrons surveyed might have about the questionnaire.

The survey team found that such outside factors as weather, football games, or major campus events, occasionally caused the actual number of patrons who utilised the catalogue room during a survey hour to drop below the estimated number of patrons who would use the card catalogue as listed in the sampling procedure. To obtain the desired twenty completed questionnaires per hour on these few occasions, the survey team reduced the interval between sampling units, or patrons, by one. Questionnaires were given to each (a–1)th patron, so that, for example, in an hour when every fifth patron was to have been given a questionnaire, one

However, he was observed discretely from a distance. The amount of time spent at the catalogue and the number of catalogue drawers searched were noted on the interview record. As the user was leaving the catalogue area, he was stopped again and asked whether his search had been successful. If the answer was affirmative, he was asked to let the interviewer copy any call numbers that he had found in the catalogue that satisfied his search needs. Users who were not certain whether their searches had been successful, but who were going elsewhere in the library to find out (usually these were people who had identified a potentially useful stack area by finding some representative class numbers in the catalogue and who intended to browse the stack for known and/or unknown documents) were given a self-mailing follow-up form on which they could conveniently note any call numbers that were subsequently found to satisfy their needs.

4 Objectivity in Study

Several months were spent at Yale in developing and testing the interview outline and technique before starting the full year's run of data collection for the project. Only very minor changes were made as the year progressed. Five individuals performed practically all of the interviews. A comparison of the results of interviews conducted by different interviewers was made about four months after the start of the interviewing year; no serious biasing of results could be associated with the interviewers compared. Therefore the interviewing technique was judged to be quite objective, as had been hoped.

The interviewing schedule that was adopted at Yale provided for a maximum of some 2,700 interviews during the full year studied. Because of various random factors (for example, no user at the catalogue at the scheduled time and place, unexpected library closings, or illness of the interviewer), the number of interviews actually completed in the year was 2,134.

5 Findings

The numerous tables and charts in the two studies document the findings from their work. I have a series of slides which highlight these findings which it would be appropriate to show at this time.

51 Traffic Pattern

The traffic studies in the Lipetz study are unique and deserve special attention. Both the figures for catalogue use *and* borrowing are remarkably similar. They both show only two significant seasons: the regular academic year, and the summer vacation period. The activity pattern of the regular academic year is punctuated by irregular declines that are associated with holidays and recesses, but the mean and median for the academic year appear to be very close. Even so, Dr Lipetz felt that the complexity of the traffic pattern strongly justified the original decision to conduct interviews throughout an entire year, with representative coverage of different days of the week, hours of the day, periods within the hour, and portals of entry to the catalogue area.

A clear pattern of the catalogue traffic variation with day of the week was observed, however. It can be seen that the rate of use of the catalogue is heaviest during the early part of the week, especially on Tuesdays, and that it is lowest on Saturdays and Sundays, as one would expect.

52 User Status

Both studies found that more use is made of the library card catalogue by graduate students than by other classes of users.

Faculty rank below undergraduates and graduate students in terms of absolute use of the catalogue.

53 Objectives of Use of Catalogue

Most of the users seek a known item at the card catalogue. The Yale study differentiated between four basic types of objectives in using the catalogue:

1 In a *document search* (often called a "known item" search), the catalogue user is aware of the existence of some particular book or other publication that he wants to locate;

2 In a *subject search,* the catalogue user is interested in both identifying and locating one or more documents pertaining to some known topic;

3 In an *author search,* the catalogue user is aware of the name of some author, publisher's series, or other source of literature and is interested in identifying and possibly selecting specific documents from that source; and

4 In a *bibliographic search,* the catalogue user is interested in using the catalogue itself to supply or verify bibliographic information regarding a known document; he is not interested in locating and using the document.

The distribution of searches among these four basic types is given in Table 1. The distribution was determined in two different ways, yielding two different results. The first column is based on the *immediate* objective of the catalogue user at the moment of his approach to the catalogue. Most of the questions asked during an interview pertained to this immediate objective. The distribution of *underlying* objectives is given in the second column of Table 1.

531 Table 1. *Distribution of Search Objectives*

Search Type	Immediate, %	Underlying, %
Document	73	56
Subject	16	33
Author	6	6
Bibliographic	5	5
	100	100

About a third of the catalogue users are basically interested in subject or topical information, but that half of these users attempt to use a document search to make do for a subject search. In terms of underlying interest, document searches account for only 56 per cent (not 73 per cent) of catalogue use.

It is interesting to note that no significant variations in the distribution of search objectives with respect to season of the year, academic status of user, departmental affiliation, or newness to the Yale library were detected in this study.

54 Other Findings at Michigan

The group at Michigan analysed their data a

little differently and came up with the following findings: The card catalogue is used primarily for academic purposes.

1 The catalogue is used most heavily for preparing class assignments.

2 Few patrons use the catalogue as a source of bibliographical data.

3 Few users seek foreign language materials; the proportion of users seeking them increases as the educational level increases.

55 Failure of Search

Both studies found that most users are successful in using the card catalogue. Only approximately 15 per cent of the searches turned up nothing at all or could be counted as unsuccessful. Yale analysed the 256 unsuccessful searches to learn more about the reasons for failure. Some 31 per cent apparently failed because of faulty search techniques or because of failure to persevere. The desired document was catalogued under entries known to the user at the time of the interview, but unfortunately he missed the clue! A table from the report shows this analysis of follow-up document searches.

56 Use of the Items of Information in an Entry

The use of different items of information on the

catalogue card was carefully analysed in both studies. The Michigan study by Palmer meticulously analysed the use of over twenty items and found that many items appearing on the catalogue card are seldom used. A hypothetical reduced computer catalogue would appear to meet the needs of most users of the card catalogue. Few users, they found at Michigan, would require more than a five-item catalogue, and the number of additional catalogue items desired increases slightly as the educational level of the patron increases.

57 Main Entry: Leading Section

The Yale study found something very interesting for anyone who has considered challenging the right of main entry to be all important in library cataloguing. Their results would seem to show that neither the name of author nor the title of document has an overwhelming advantage as candidate for the leading section of the main entry and for preferred search approach. There seems to be an advantage to the title approach, but only a slight one. One can question why there is such a strong tendency for library users to approach the catalogue by name of author if the title approach is just about as good if not better.

6 Computer-Based Catalogue

The analysis of failures in searching the catalogue could not be compensated for in computerised catalogue, unless a near-human facility compensating for inadequacies in search clues were built in. The computer will fail to select unless it is given some definite programme that will cause it to ignore particular kinds of mismatches. Until such methods are available, Dr Lipetz concluded that it seems highly unlikely that computer methods of document finding will seriously rival document finding capacity of human beings. He recommended further intensive research work on the user of our catalogues and the relative-offs in usefulness and cost of including additional data elements in a computerized record. If, as Dr Palmer at Michigan found, a five-item catalogue record suffices, then we need to study the interface between the user and such a new catalogue before we proceed much further toward library automation.

7 Improving Catalogue Use

Having learned so much about the reader in search of his book, one of the most important conclusions seems to be that user-education or self-education methods need to be improved before our libraries can give efficient service. Increasing the complexity and accessibility of the catalogue offers comparatively little potential for improvement of the success rate of searches currently attempted. Improving the convenience of the catalogue use might attract heavier use of the catalogue and the library collection. Providing access through a greater variety of title-like entries is a promising approach to helping document search. Filing by date within subject headings is a promising approach to helping search by name of subject. Data elements other than name of author, title, and subject are of most value in resolving many searches in which the entry clues are ambiguous or inaccurate.

With this much new information about the user, it is well to turn our attention to the next law of library science, and consider our techniques for every book finding its reader.

CHAPTER G

LAW 3: EVERY BOOK ITS READER — HOW EVERY BOOK BE FOUND BY ITS READER

1 Catalogue and Readers' Requirements

11 Structure of Catalogue

Cataloguers have a view of library service which in many ways is most distorted and at the same time most central. Without their efforts at bibliographic control where would library service be? Without some form of listing the items in a library, how could anyone ever find anything? Nevertheless, some people are now asking — even with the help of the cataloguer's effort, we do not seem to find what is available? Has the time come for us to carefully analyse what happens when a cataloguer performs the present ritual of describing books for readers? Many of us have embarked upon such a study only recently because the availability of MARC (Machine Readable Cataloguing) has given us access to current catalogue information in a form easy to manipulate for study. The accessibility of all the information on a catalogue card as access points instead of only three or four elements (main entry, title, subject, call number) makes it possible to match the individual user's words used in a subject search with any portion of the catalogue record allows us to study our present cataloguing rules for main and added entry and test their potency compared to other elements.

Some of us (including students in library schools, such as Syracuse) are asking:

1 Is the main entry form we establish for corporate bodies really useful to the reader in search of a particular book?

2 Is our rule for main and added entries for works by more than three authors valid if we are trying to describe a book accurately?

3 Are there other items of information on the catalogue card that are more descriptive of the book's content than the main and added entries we have established for it? If yes, shouldn't these be more accessible for the user in search of material on a given subject?

4 Is our strict control over the names of subjects we use in cataloguing essential if we maintain an integrated bibliographic retrieval system, with catalogues, name of subject authority files, and biographical reference sources available at one and the same time in the computer?

12 View as a Whole

I am not sure that we can completely uproot all

of our present practices and rules for descriptive and subject cataloguing. Nor am I sure that we can indict today's cataloguers as persons with a myopic view, that is, do they see service to users for the mountain of books still needing cataloguing. It is safe to say that their work does necessitate their view of each and every book as an entity to be handled separately. Only rarely do they get a chance to view the whole scene of which their individual effort is but a small part. Many of them view their work as assembly, or piece work. Most libraries are not equipped with aids or devices which would facilitate the work of cataloguers so that they could see the true impact on the library catalogue as they catalogue individual works. How many cataloguers know how close their description of a book comes to matching the user's clue words when he is in search of that book? The two studies I discussed in the previous lecture provide some useful information about book descriptions in card catalogues and their use by university scholars. This brings us a little closer to an awareness of this important relationship — the book and the reader — but we still have a long way to go.

2 Investigation

In this lecture I am quite proud to report on some work a few students at Syracuse have done to enlarge our understanding of this subject. With the availability of MARC tapes from the Library of Congress and some computerized retrieval programs from IBM, we were able to study cataloguing records very carefully, and compare the retrieval of books from a catalogue having traditional access points with retrieval from a catalogue with unlimited access points.

21 Marc Format

Before I begin to discuss our findings, perhaps an explanation of the MARC format is necessary. It is not important for this discussion to be very detailed in this explanation, nor for that matter, entirely up-to-date. For example, we began our work using MARC I records. This was during the MARC Pilot Project at the Library of Congress. Since March 1969, the Library of Congress has been distributing MARC II records. The MARC II format is much more elaborate in identifying and tagging fields and elements of information. Our work with MARC I records could also be done with MARC II records, if we chose. For the purposes of our study, however, which format we used was not as important as the information content. It was the content of a Library of Congress catalogue card, created by cataloguers following the rules for main entry, descriptive cataloguing, subject cataloguing and classification that we were scrutinizing. What they created was now accessible in ways they never

MARC Pilot Project
Bibliographic Listing

0) LC Card No. 66–018912

Filed Field Information :

					Supplement	*Conference*	*Juvenile*
1) *Type of Entry*	2) *Form of Work*	3) *Biblio*	4) *Illus*	5) *Maps*	6) Number	7) Conference	8) Work
Personal Author	Monograph	Yes	None	None	None	No	No

9) *Language Data*: 10) *Publication Data*:

Class	*Lang 1*	*Lang 2*	*Key*	*Date 1*	*Date 2*	*Place*	*Name*	*Height*
Translation	Eng	Unk	Single	1966		NYNY	PGR	21CM

Name of Variable Field	*Tag*	
Main Entry	10	Mao, Tse-Tung, 1893-1
Title Statement	20	Basic Tactics. Translated and with an Introd. By Stuart R Schram. Foreword by Samuel B Griffith II
Imprint Statement	30	New York, PRAEGER 1966
Collation Statement	40	VIII, 149 P. 21 CM
Notes	60	Bibliographical Footnotes.
Subject Tracing	70	Guerrilla Warfare.
Pers Author Tracing	71	Schram, Stuart R, Ed and Tr
Title Tracing	74	T
L C Call Number	90	U240.M28 1966
Dewey Class Number	91	355.425

Mao, Tse-tung, 1893—
Basic tactics. Translated and with an introd by Stuart R Schram. Foreword by Samuel. B Griffith, II. New York, Praeger [1966]-

viii, 149p. 21 cm.

Bibliographical footnotes.

1 Guerrilla warfare I. Schram, Stuart R. and tr. II. Title
U240.M28 355.425 66-1891
Library of Congress

imagined, and we were curious to find out how useful their descriptions of books were for machine searching.

The figure of a MARC I record explained and set beside the printed catalogue card for Mao Tse-tung's book entitled *Basic tactics,* shows how every field of information on the catalogue card is not only analysed but explicitly tagged.

In the actual machine readable record on magnetic tape or punched cards, the field tag 10 would appear directly before the main entry line, field tag 20 would appear before the title statement, tag 70 would appear before the subject entry, tag 90 before the Library of Congress call number, and tag 92 before the Dewey class number. Additional information about the work in hand is described in coded fashion, in what are called fixed-length fields. For example, in character position 21 on the MARC I record, a code would appear which indicated the type of main entry. For example, Mao Tse-tung is a personal main entry. Therefore, the code P would appear in character position 21. If the book's main entry were a government body, a code letter G would appear in character position 21, S for Society, R for Religious body, T for Title main entry, and so on. If the notes section of the catalogue card made reference to a bibliography, there would be an X in character position 23. On this figure all of these fixed field codes have been translated for ease of use of the reader. For example, the listing reads "yes" under *Biblio* in the Fixed Field portion. This is a translation of the coded information on the MARC record, indicating that there is an "X" in character position 23.

211 *Reformatted Marc Record*

When we reformatted the MARC records for use with the IBM Document Processing System, we knew that *every* group of characters on the MARC record bounded on either side by spaces would be considered a keyword, accessible for searching. That meant that the Dewey Class Number was a Keyword, by definition. So was every word in the title statement including *and, with, by* (unless we instructed the computer to ignore them as common words). This also meant that every word in a subject heading was now a keyword, not only the first word as is true in our catalogues. As if through a glass darkly, I saw the first glimmerings of something like a classified catalogue approach available to American Library users! Is this too big a concept to grasp over so many miles? The workings of the computer program for accessing the information on the MARC records is fairly complicated, but the use of the MARCS/DPS system as we called it was not — luckily. All that the user needed to do was to structure his searches in English-like sentences, combining keywords with logical operators (such as *and, or*), availing himself of some useful modifiers or delimiters. He could for example specify that two keywords had to be side-by-side in a MARC record or he should not want to see the record. He could specify which field (or sentence) to search for his particular keyword. This was very useful when searching the file by using Dewey class numbers as keywords. A three-digit Dewey number looks like any other three-digit number to the computer, and we knew that the collation contained the number of pages in a book, and numbers appeared elsewhere. By phrasing his search in the following way, he could exclude any three-digit numbers other than those in the Dewey Class number field:

L1 355 ($);
L2 L1 AND T92(SEN);

We knew that the field tag numbers would be confounded with other two-digit numbers when the MARC record was processed by the Document Processing System, so we instructed the computer programmer to insert the letter T before every field tag number. This gave us a group of unique keywords representing the MARC field tags.

3 Library Education Experimental Project

31 Facility

With such a laboratory facility at our disposal, we proceeded to study catalogue records and test the finding of books by new search strategies. We called this laboratory LEEP (Library Education Experimental Project). During its first year-and-a-half, it was supported by the U S Office of Education. Now it is maintained by Syracuse University as an integral part of the educational facilities available to students and faculty in the School of Library Science.

32 Sample Catalogue

For the studies reported here in detail we used a sample catalogue of approximately 10,000 books in the social sciences, representing titles published primarily in 1967-68. It was a stratified sample of the larger MARC Pilot Project file of approximately 48,000 titles. We were able to create such a sample by computer manipulation of the file because we had analysed the content of the entire file during the earlier stages of LEEP.

33 Major Objective

Most of the projects the library school students developed centred around the third question I asked at the outset of this lecture: Are there other fields of information on the catalogue card that are more descriptive of the book's content than the main and added entries we have established for it?

If the answer was found to be yes we intended to tell the world of librarianship so they could begin to consider making such data more accessible. This new information, we felt, would help justify library automation and MARC records not on the basis of efficiency of library operations but on the basis of the third law of library science, namely *every book its reader.*

34 Searches

Many students, more than two hundred in fact, performed searches using MARCS/DPS. They performed these searches while they were students in reference and bibliography classes, cataloguing and technical services classes, or in advanced courses in information systems. Several students went beyond one or two searches, and two of them organised their work into a small research study and wrote down their findings in a fashion suitable for publication. One report is in the process of being published by *Library resources and technical services* and the second is almost ready for submission to the *Journal of the American Society for Information Science*. My report of their work will be the first public report. I have their permission to report their work to you and I am indeed proud to do so.

4 Study 1

41 Objective

One student, Mrs Judith Hudson was interested in finding all the relevant information in the MARCS/DPS file for *area studies* bibliographies. This is not a simple matter in a traditional card catalogue and she was not sure which would be the most efficient way to find documents in a machine-based catalogue, such a MARCS/DPS. She set out to:

1 Discover the optimum search strategy to find at least 95% of the relevant documents in our computer-based catalogue on an area of the world;

2 Discover what other methods to use if one search strategy is not optimum; and

3 Determine why non-relevant document references would be found.

If possible, she hoped that her study would allow her to recommend search strategies which would minimize "false drops" and maximize "hits."

42 Definition

The first step in constructing the searches was to begin defining terms and geographic areas. Area studies or area research are considered to be "the interdisciplinary study of a given geographic region, country or group of countries (considered as a unit), which takes account of the socially significant data about the area, including the history of the people, their economic and political development and their use of natural resources" (24). "Area studies ... may treat the topography, ethnography, natural resources, religion, sociology, economy, law, government, history, culture (or any combination of these) for an area, large or small" (23).

The area to be studied was the Middle East. Later on in the study, it was decided to examine another area as a check on the results of the Middle East Study. Latin America was chosen.

It was decided that "the Arab countries, inclusive of North Africa, together with Israel, Turkey, Iran and Afghanistan — often called collectively the Near East or Middle East ... constitute a regional unit" (4). Latin America was defined as "that part of the Western hemisphere that lies south of the border of the United States and of the Florida Strait. It includes Middle America (Mexico, Central America and the West Indies) and South America" (3).

43 Search Strategy

In order to find all the relevant MARC records from the file, four different types of searches were written:

1 Searches for keywords — English language words and phrases — for example, Middle East, Palestine, etc.

2 Searches for *Library of Congress* (L C) *Classification* numbers on the area — for example, DS36, F1869, etc.

3 Searches for *Dewey Classification* numbers on the area — for example, 956, 972, etc.

4 *"If-scan" searches* — The "If-scan" function enables the user to scan a specified field of the Record portion of the MARC/DPS record for a given character or character string. In this case, we specified that the computer scan the field called DDCNO, which is the Dewey Classification number, for an area code. Such a search for the area code 56 (Middle East) would yield such Dewey numbers as 560, 956, 321.00956, etc.

44 Preparation for Search

441 *Search by Keyword*

The first step in preparing the keyword searches was to compile a list of words and phrases which would yield records relevant to an area study. We examined the Dewey and L C Classification Schedules for the two areas and listed all of the relevant words and phrases we could find. To this list were added such words as geographical names, names of religions, and famous people representative of the area, etc. Each word and phrase was checked in our index list of keywords in MARCS/DPS to see if the word appeared in the file of 8,000 MARC records. If a word was not listed in this index, it was discarded.

The words which remained formed the *keyword searches*. They were combined according to DPS vocabulary and syntax rules in such a way as to find every MARC record which contained any one or more of the specified words or phrases regardless of where it might appear in the text portion.

442 *Search by Class Number*

The L C and Dewey Classification searches were prepared by examining the L C and Dewey schedules to determine the appropriate class number on the area. These class numbers were checked in the 'index list'. If they appeared in this index, the DPS search was written to find every MARC record which contained the specified L C or Dewey Classification numbers.

443 *"If-scan" Search*

The "If-scan" search was prepared for the applicable area notations from the Dewey Classification Area Table (2). All MARC records having a Dewey class number built with these area notations were to be retrieved.

45 Examples

Searches were run on MARCS/DPS. The Middle East searches were as follows:

451 *Keyword Searches*

Search Number 206

L1 DEAD & SEA(+1);
L2 MOUNT & CARMEL(+1);
L3 TEL & AVIV(+1);
L4 IBN & SAUD(+1);
L5 BENI & KURT(+1);
L6 PALESTINE, ISRAEL, JORDAN, ARAB($);
L7 ANTIOCH, PALMYRA, SMYRNA, SUMERIANS, TYRE, UR;
L8 JEW($), JERUSALEM, BETHLEHEM, EMMAUS, MEGIDDO, NAZARETH;
L9 NEGEV, NEGEB, CAPPADOCIA, HEROD, HUSSEIN, JUDEA, AFGHANISTAN;
L10 L6 & T10 (NOT SEN);
L11 PERGAMON & T30 (NOT SEN);
L12 MEDINA, DARIUS, BAHRAMPOUR, ISMAIL, MAHMUD;
L13 L1, L2, L3, L4, L5, L6, L7, L8, L9, L10, L11, L12;

LIST OFFLINE, TEXT, SUBJECTS

Search Number 207

L1 MIDDLE & EAST(+1);
L2 NEAR & EAST(+1);
L3 UNITED & ARAB(+1) & REPUBLIC (+1);
L4 TURKEY, TURKS, CYPRUS, SYRIA, LEBANON;
L5 IRAQ, IRAN, PERSIAN, MESOPOTAMIA, EGYPT($);
L6 ASIA & MINOR(+1);
L7 MOROCCO, ALGERIA($), TUNIS($), LIBYA, SUDAN;
L8 ARMENIA, ISLAM($), BEDOUIN;
L9 EUPHRATES, ANATOLIA, ANKARA, ARARAT, ADEN, MOSQUE, MUSLIM ($);
L10 BABYLON($), KURDISH, KISH, BEIRUT, LEVANT;
L11 L1, L2, L3, L4, L5, L6, L7, L8, L9, L10;

LIST OFFLINE, TEXT, SUBJECTS;

452 *L C Searches*

Search Number 208

L1 DS1($), DS2($), DS313($), DS326($), DS38($), DS43.S5,DS44($), DS48. F53, DS49($);

DS53($), DS62($), DS70.6($),
DS71.07($), DS80.9($), DS84($),
DS89.T($);

L3 DS99($);

L4 L1, L2, L3;

LIST OFFLINE, TEXT, LCCALL:

453 *Dewey Searches*

Search Number 209

L1 915.6($), 955($), 956($);

L2 L1 & T92(SEN);

LIST OFFLINE, TEXT, DDCNO;

46 RECORD OF SEARCH RESULT

The method used for recording the information gathered in the searches was straightforward: Once run, each of the searches resulted in a print-out, with statistics and document references which met the search criteria. Each MARC record in the MARC/DPS file has a unique number and that document number was used for identification of individual MARC records.

Each MARC record selected was examined and the following information was recorded:

1 Document number;

2 Is it relevant (R), questionable (Q), or not relevant (NR)?;

3 Search number;
4 Kind of search; and
5 Keyword(s) which caused the record to be selected.

For keyword searches other than LC or Dewey class numbers, the location (by MARC tag number) where the keyword appeared was recorded. For example, here's one document reccrd:

Doc No 4469		RXQ NR
Search No	Kind	KW
208	LC	DS 80.9
209	DC	956.92
210	IFSc	956.92
207	KW	Lebanon

Side 1 (*For side* 2 *see next page*)

47 FINDINGS

The findings of Mrs Hudson's study are a little startling for any of us who hoped to prove that searching the file by class number would be more

Doc No 4469					
KW	T10	T20	T60	T70	Other
Lebanon		X		X	

Side 2

useful than any other keyword approach. The following table points up how few relevant documents were found using either the L C or D C numbers, when compared to keywords found anywhere in the MARC record.

AREA : MIDDLE EAST

Search Strategy	Relevant Hits	Precision ratio R ret / T ret	Recall Ratio R ret / Total R
KW	101	40.6%	97.1%
LC	36	14.4	34.6
DC	26	10.4	25.0
IF Sc	21	8.8	20.1
KW & LC	103	41.3	99
KW & DC	103	41.3	99
KW & IF SC	102	40.9	98
KW & LC & DC	104	41.7	100

AREA : LATIN AMERICA

Search Strategy	Relevant Hits	Precision ratio R found / T found	Recall ratio R found / Total R
KW	143	33.4%	98.6%
LC	60	14.1	41.3
DC	47	11.0	32.4
IF SC	36	8.4	24.8
KW & LC	145	33.9	100
KW & DC	144	33.7	99.4
KW & IF SC	143	33.4	98.6
KW & LC & DC	145	33.9	100

471 *Annotation*

Total R is 104 (Middle East), 145 (Latin America)

T found for any single search strategy is the sum of documents found using it alone or in any combination with other strategies.

48 Analysis of Findings

The analysis of the placement of the keywords in the MARC record is at the heart of the problem. Where do the keyword hits and false drops come from? The table on page 106 tells an interesting story which looks consistent for area studies searches

KEYWORDS IN DATA FIELD	MIDDLE EAST			LATIN AMERICA		
	RELE-VANT	QUES-TION-ABLE	NON-RE-LEVANT	RELE-VANT	QUES-TION-ABLE	NON-RE-LEVANT
Single field hits:						
T10 (author)	0	0	9	0	0	11
T20 (title)	8	1	12	9	5	15
T30 (imprint)	0	3	11	0	1	10
T60 (notes)	2	2	3	3	2	16
T70 (subject heading)	19	1	7	16	5	5
Hits in more than one field:						
T20/T70 (title and subject heading)	70	0	7	49	4	15
T20/T60/T70 (title, noter and subject heading)	9	0	0	7	0	1

Table 4: Keyword Hits by MARC Data Field

for two parts of the world. The fields for author and imprint often yielded non-relevant reference, or false drops. These same fields were never the only reason for the retrieval of a relevant MARC record. It appeared that keyword searches restricted to fields for the title, series notes, notes, and subject headings eliminated many false drops without sacrificing the finding of any relevant records. The table also shows that the fields for title *and* subject heading (T20 and T70 in the MARC I records respectively) are the most effective for finding relevant documents. Keywords in the title field can be both useful and a nuisance, according to these findings.

To find documents on an area of the world, then, we concluded that the keyword search seems optimum, with the use of L C numbers and then Dewey class numbers following for exhaustivity. The homonym problem caused a great many false drops during such searches and seems unavoidable with an "uncontrolled" vocabulary of keyword searching such as that done in MARC/DPS. For example, Israel (the country) and Israel (the surname) cannot be distinguished.

491 *Conclusion*

Mrs Hudson concluded her papers as follows: The fact that keyword searches were better than searches using a classification system was not surprising. Material on a given geographic area is not easily found on the shelf in any library. It is scattered because other aspects of the material are highlighted and used for primary subject access. The subdivisions of subject headings, more than the geographical codes in D C, appear to provide access to some of this material. To access the subdivisions, however, a catalogue record must be in machine readable form and the programming system used for searching the records must allow access to any word in the subject field, not just the first word. MARC/DPS is such a system. Our results show that two MARC I fields (title and subject) provide access to the relevant documents for an area study search. Neither is sufficient alone.

We are not certain that our findings hold true for other kinds of subject searches (for example, biographical, political, historical, literary, etc). Much more work along the lines described here will have to be done before the class numbers (either L C or D C) on MARC records should be discarded as subject access points in a mechanized document finding system. Before we can say that the title and subject heading fields should be considered the primary routes of subject access to library materials, someone will have to test the entire system more rigorously than we have here.

5 Study 2

51 Objectives

Michael Ubaldini, a recent graduate of the School of Library Science at Syracuse University, delved a little more deeply into MARC searching than Mrs Hudson. He refined some of the objectives of her work and pinpointed for very close scrutiny the placement of keywords in various MARC fields. He had eight objectives when he undertook his research:

1 To analyse *keyword searches* (phase 1) to determine if there were any well-defined *relationships* between finding relevant documents and specifying which tagged MARC fields should be searched.

2 If such relationships existed, to determine if an increase in the *precision ratio* could be effected by such field specification.

3 If so, to determine the subsequent effect on the *total estimated recall.*

4 If the effect on the total estimated recall was favourable, to determine the sequence in which the tagged fields should be searched to insure high precision and equally high recall.

5 To determine the effect of restricting searches to *single fields*; to compare these results with *multiple-field* searching; and to conclude which method,

if either, is better for obtaining high precision and recall.

6 To determine what part, if any, the following *search characteristics* played in the question of tagged field specification: subject area searched, search author, length and degree of specificity of the search.

7 To construct keyword, L C, and D C searches (phase 2) on one topic to *test* the results of phase 1 (steps 1–6 above).

8 To compare the results concerning tagged field specification of Judy Hudson's report on *area studies* with the results of his work and to determine if her recommendations could be extended to all *keyword* searches.

The concept of single-field versus *multiple-field* searches is an important one. Some document finding systems allow selection only by single-field keyword occurrences. The KWIC indexing of article *title words* (analogous to field T20 in the MARC I records) is an example. It allows access to the contents of these articles solely by the indexing of keywords in the titles of the articles indexed. This may, in fact, be desirable. Allowing specified keywords to be indexed and accessed from multiple parts of an article (for example, abstract, affiliation) may cause the finding of many irrelevant drops,

TABLE 8: *Unique* documents found by *single-field* keyword occurrences (Analogous to KWIC indexing)

FIELD	Total Docs found	Relevant	Non-rel.	Quest.	Precision Ratio %	T Estimated Recall %
T10 (main entry)	4	3	0	1	75	3
T20 (title)	36	30	5	1	83	27
T30 (imprint)	4	0	4	0	0	0
T40 (collation)	0	–	–	–	–	–
T51 (series)	3	0	3	0	0	0
T60 (notes)	9	6	3	0	67	5
T70 (subject headings)	32	23	6	3	72	21
T7 + (corporate author)	6	1	5	0	16	1
T80 (copy information)	0	–	–	–	–	–
TOTAL RESULTS	79	51R	23N	5Q	65	48

TABLE 9: Documents found by *multiple-field* keyword occurrences (Phase I results)

FIELD	Total Docs found	Relevant	Non-rel.	Quest.	Precision Ratio %	T Estimated Recall %
T10 (main entry)	27	13	10	4	48	12
T20 (title)	122	78	30	14	64	70
T30 (imprint)	20	9	8	3	45	8
T40 (collation)	2	2	0	0	100	2
T51 (series)	25	5	18	2	20	5
T60 (notes)	59	30	20	9	51	27
T70 (subject headings)	107	76	19	12	71	69
T7 + (corporate author)	28	10	17	1	36	9
T80 (copy information)	1	1	0	0	100	1
TOTAL RESULTS*	162	95	44	23	59	86

* These total results do not represent the arithmetic sums of their respective columns because one keyword may have appeared in many fields of a document retrieved by the keyword strategy.

TABLE 10: Documents found by *multiple-field* keyword occurrence (Phase 2 results)

	Total	Documents Retrieved			Precision Ratio %	Total Est. Recall %
		Relevant	Non-rel.	Quest.		
Documents retrieved by *all* strategies	43	14	20	9	33	100
Documents retrieved by *keywords*	19	12	1	6	63	86
Documents retrieved by *LC* class nos	16	6	8	2	38	43
Documents retrieved by *DC* class nos	23	10	12	1	44	72
Field (s) specified for keyword search						
T10 (main entry)	0	–	–	–	–	–
T20 (title)	6	5	0	1	83	36
T30 (imprint)	0	–	–	–	–	–
T40 (collation)	0	–	–	–	–	–
T51 (series)	0	–	–	–	–	–
T60 (notes)	3	1	1	1	33	7
T70 (subject headings)	15	11	0	4	73	79
T80 (copy information)	0	–	–	–	–	–
T20 or T70	16	11	0	5	69	79
T20 or T60 or T70	19	12	1	6	63	86
T10 or T20 or T60 or T70						
T20 or T30 or T60 or T70	19	12	1	6	63	86

but may insure a substantially higher number of additional relevant documents to be selected.

52 FINDINGS

Ubaldini's findings show interesting differences if single-field searches are compared with multiple-field searches.

53 CONCLUSION

He summarised his results as follows:

1 Analysis of the table of single-field keyword occurrences indicates that the most useful fields for finding *relevant* MARC records may be ranked as follows:

T20 (title)
T70 (subject headings)
T60 (notes)
T10 (main entry)

The ranking would be different if the precision ratio were used as the sole criterion because the number of non-relevant retrievals in these fields varies.

2 Analysis of the table of multiple-field keyword occurrences supports the validity of this sequence. The table which records the results of the test keyword search (phase 2), shows that all 12 relevant documents were retrieved by specifying only fields T20, T60 and T70 to be searched.

3 Single-field keyword searching was not as effective as multiple-field searching. 79 of a possible 162 documents were retrieved by the single-field keyword strategy. Of these 79 documents, 51 were assessed as relevant (a precision ratio of 65 per cent). By allowing keyword occurrence in all fields, 95 relevant documents were retrieved (a precision ratio of 59 per cent). Multiple-field retrievals gave a slightly lower precision ratio, but the increase in the total estimated recall was critical, an increase from 48 per cent to 86 per cent. This would mean, for example, that a KWIC indexing of all the fields of the MARC record would furnish less than half of the relevant documents in the data base while multiple-field searching would furnish over 6/7 of the relevant documents. From another viewpoint, allowing multiple-field searching nearly doubled the total number of relevant documents retrieved, with little cost to the overall precision.

4 Using MARCS/DPS, relevant documents were selected by the occurrence of one or more of a number of specified keywords in the *titles* of these documents (field T20). Manually searching an alphabetically arranged card catalogue by the title of a document would have selected only those documents which had a specified keyword as the *first word* of its title. Analysis of the first indexable word of a sample of 20 relevant documents

selected by searches analysed in this report indicates that only 40 per cent of these documents would be retrieved by a manual search of a card catalogue which contained entries for these documents. That is, for the searches studied here, approximately only 28 per cent of the total number of relevant documents in the card catalogue would be selected by a manual search compared to the retrieval of 70 per cent by use of computer access.

5 Using MARCS/DPS allowed the keyword searching of the *notes* portion of a catalogue entry (field T60). Some of the documents selected in this study could not have been found by a manual search of a card catalogue under title or subject heading. One example is the case of a compilation of articles in which the article titles are given in the notes. A few of the documents retrieved by the search on Shakespearean drama, for example, were retrieved solely by keyword occurrence in the notes. In the light of the results of this report, the ability to search this part of a catalogue entry for specified keywords may be a very valuable facility.

6 In summary, when one considers the title, notes, and subject entries, the occurrence of specified keywords in these fields taken together rather than in any *one* of these fields alone, the total number of relevant documents found is increased by

26 per cent while the precision ratio is decreased by only 3 per cent.

6 Comparison of Findings

The following statement of Mrs Hudson is corroborated by the results of Mr Ubaldini's report: "The fields for *title* and *subject heading* (T20 and T70 respectively) are the most effective for retrieving relevant MARC records." However, her statement that the "author, imprint, and title fields (T10, T30. and T20 respectively) account for most of the non-relevant keyword hits," may not be extended to all keyword searches as is evidenced by the analyses in Ubaldini's report.

In her report, Mrs Hudson recommends that the following fields be searched to obtain high precision and recall in an area study: "filing or conventional title (T15), title statement (T20), series, traced (T50), series, not traced (T51), notes (T60), and subject headings (T70)." The results of Ubaldini's report do not confirm the wholesale extension of her recommendations for area studies to all keyword searches. They do confirm the searching of fields title, notes, and subject. However, since *no* keyword occurrences in his study were noted in fields for conventional title or series (traced), it is not expedient to recommend that they be searched in all keyword searches. In his report, field

T51 (series, not traced) was responsible for retrieving 3 documents (all non-relevant) by single-field keyword occurrence and 25 documents (18 non-relevant) by multiple-field keyword occurrence. In multiple-field searches, T51 was responsible for selecting 5 relevant documents, all of which would have been selected anyway if field T51 had been excluded from being searched. Therefore, the recommendation that field T51 be searched in an area study does not appear to be easily extended to all keyword searches.

7 Remarks

Ubaldini's conclusions have great impact on the future of cataloguing as we know it today. If we are to continue to obey the third law, it is possible that we will have to revise our practices quite dramatically. We cannot ignore much longer such statements as the following: The most productive fields for subject searching, as determined by the results of this report, are title, notes and subject headings. Specifying additional MARC fields for searching will either result in (a) a greater decrease in precision with little increase in recall, or (b) the selection of *no* additional MARC records.

Requiring that all the keywords (specified in a search) be found in a single field *critically reduces* the number of relevant MARC records selected by the search. The resulting recall ratio is likely to be lower than is desired by the users of the system.

The use of L C subject headings as a means of access to catalogue entries of monographs may not be as useful as is generally accepted. It appears, from the results of this report, that a KWIC index of the monograph titles for specified keywords would have selected a greater number of relevant MARC records than searching the subject headings for these keywords, without appreciably lowering the precision ratio of the search. The necessity for L C subject headings in the MARC record is put in serious doubt. Nevertheless, the results of this report also point to the conclusion that searching the subject heading field *in addition to* the title and notes fields did select many more relevant records than searching the titles and subject headings alone.

CHAPTER H

LAW 4: SAVE THE TIME OF THE READER A PLEA FOR UNITED ACTION!

1 A Measure of Efficiency

In the one hundred years since Melvil Dewey and Charles Ammi Cutter were young librarians, we have erected a great many devices for bibliographic control. The studies I reviewed in earlier lectures are a few of the recent attempts to find whether these devices assist or prevent the reader's access to the documents he seeks. These studies have just scratched the surface of what we need to know about the match between a user's information needs and the systematic description of our information resources — the documents.

In communications research, they speak of the *gatekeeper function*. Library catalogues are a form of gate in the communication process between reader and book, and cataloguers and reference librarians are gatekeepers of a sort. By what criterion do we measure the performance of our task? I submit that the fourth Law of Library Science should be used. In constructing the catalogue and other library tools, do we save the time of the reader or do we add to the time he must spend before he can put to use the information resources we have collected for his use? Many studies in libraries centre around increased efficiency of the library staff in performing certain functions, but very few are cost/effectiveness studies of the information seeker.

2 Making Students' Experience It

As a feeble attempt to make library science students aware of the need to evaluate our functions in this light, I usually require beginning students in cataloguing to chart their own path of information seeking from known information need to information satisfaction. They measure the steps and the minutes it takes to go from their study desk to an index or the library catalogue, to the book shelf or circulation desk, and finally to the book itself. It is usually a revelation to them when they add up the steps and can count their efforts in hundreds of feet, when they add up the minutes and can see that one such search took almost a half-hour! After this, they seem to take much more interest in "saving the time of the reader" and they also seem to have this law uppermost in their minds whenever we discuss anything which may set up hurdles for the user. For example, the establishment of main entry for corporate bodies or conference proceedings always bothers a new class in cataloguing because a comparison of the title page and the catalogue card shows very few common elements, oftentimes. They ask, "How can we continue to do this and still say we are saving the time of the reader who has a known item in mind?" Needless to say, I am at a loss for words on such occasions and quickly switch the subject to automated library catalogues where, I hope, we will have freer access to all the information we store.

3 Focus on the Reader

31 Designing for Better Use

It is not an easy problem to solve. How can we measure our present efforts to save the time of the reader (and the staff) when the library is such a complex organisation and no one function can be changed without having a rippling effect throughout the organisation? We can begin at one obvious place, in my opinion. We can begin to concentrate on knowing more about the reader. This awareness will force us to design or redesign our information centres and libraries to facilitate their use. This new point of view (new for many) can effectively transform many libraries with no real modernisation effort such as automation being necessary. I have visited many public libraries in the United States, in large cities and small towns, and I always enter the building with the fourth law on my mind. I murmur to myself, "How does this library save the time of the reader?" By observing where the information signs are, where the librarian sits, where the card catalogue stands, where the book return is located, how a reader signs out a book, and how the catalogue user is aided in his search, I can tell very easily if the library is enforcing the fourth law. Equipment is not the only essential to save the time of the reader. The spirit of willingness to serve or to help the reader help himself is more essential.

32 Subjective Time

More than the 'objective time', the 'subjective time' of the reader is important. While waiting in a queue to use a particular catalogue drawer, or to get a book charged or discharged, although the objective time may be only a couple of minutes, it might appear as waiting for hours for the busy reader. Even an additional minute he takes to find the appropriate catalogue entry for his document can increase his impatience and frustration. This is true also of locating a document on the shelves using the call number, etc. This subjective time varies from reader to reader and even with one and the same reader from one context to another.

4 Principle of Least Action

When I became interested in the use of computers for information storage and retrieval, I noticed how easily this fourth law could be ignored even though increased efficiency was supposedly the objective of the system. Don Swanson said in the February 1966 issue of the *Bulletin of the atomic scientists* that "the design of any information service should be predicated on the assumption that its customers will exert minimal effort in order to receive its benefits." Users of such services, he said, operate under *the principle of least action.* If this be so, then we must take the user into account every day of our existence and be sure that every attempt is made to save his time as well as our own. The problem is one of organisation, not of computerisation. The conference on library and information networks in my country, which I spoke of in the first lecture (Chapter E, Sec 4) placed more importance on agreements to effect compatibility, combinability, and multiple use of records than on any other problem. We may consider it inefficient to type catalogue cards for the same book that was catalogued before in another library, but imagine the poor reader who must use several different bibliographical sources only to come up with a list of known items which he must now trace through several different libraries. Without union lists and greater cooperation between librarians and publishers of indexes, bibliographies, etc, we add enormous workloads to the users of our services.

5 Standarisation and Simplification

I must apologise because I do not know too much about the efforts in India to save the time of the reader and the staff in your information centres, but when I surveyed efforts in the United States a few years ago, I had to conclude that there has been no concerted effort on the part of any group to be wholly or even partly in tune with anyone else in producing compatible tools, easily combinable for bibliographical reference work. Title abbreviations for serials, for example, differ in different reference works; libraries create union lists of serials with no aids to ease this problem. It is as if we were building railroads, each on a different gauge track so that no equipment or trains could pass from one company's tracks to another.

A research team from System Development Corporation painted even a blacker picture in their report to the US Federal Council for Science and Technology, Committee on Scientific and Technical Information:

"Unless someone with unusual foresight and influence establishes workable standardisation, the history of library coordination as a mechanisable system complex may be as turbulent as the history of higher-order computer languages has been. Unfortunately, the rush of library automa-

> tion efforts could be so rapid that each installation, preoccupied with attaining its own internal efficiency, might not notice the incompatibilities of its formats, codes, etc, with those of other libraries unless strong efforts — such as those that a capping agency could exert — are made to coordinate these aspects of library automation" (22).

It is possible that the users of our tools and libraries may solve their problems in their own way, and we may not be called upon to help. But should we sit passively and wait to be called to help? I think not, if we adhere to the fourth law. Don Swanson suggests that information systems should provide for more digestion, summary, and packing down of knowledge, which will permit the library user to progress without floundering in the backlog of published information. He states categorically:

> "Most present libraries and information systems wait to be used. A modern information system, however, should seek out its customers . . . we infer that these systems will provide de-centralised service points and selective, direct, and continuous distribution of information to customers. Service in response to standing requests should be maximised, so that customer initiative can be minimised" (21).

6 Points for Consideration

With such words to guide us, we must ask ourselves: Are we following the fourth law? More specifically we might ask: What are we doing to effect a positive plan to meet the following needs:

1 We need to stress a coordinated approach to information system and network development — from *origin* of information (author's manuscript to editor/publisher) to *use* of information (in library, research worker's office and the like).

2 We need to combine efforts and avoid *redo* of input operations (automatic typesetting for publisher; machine-readable cataloguing for library; data compilations in information centres).

3 We should follow the *principle of least action* in information systems for every library user.

4 We should follow the *principle of by-product data* generation in machine-generated data.

5 We must make *provision for combinability and flexibility* of information records.

7 Cooperation

71 Work Together

For all these projects, we need to work together across state and national borders and across *library* border. We need a unifying force — provided by some governmental authority or by our own professional zeal to accomplish our stated goals. Dr Ranganathan in his life-time of work, shows us the way, but now we collectively must do what one man tried to do single-handed forty years ago. Our task is more difficult because we do not have a unifying body-force he has. Can we strive for it? Let us share the ideas about how to begin.

72 Holistic Approach

There is another sense in which united action or integrated effort is essential. The requirements and psychology of readers are complex; they are dynamic and changing. No single tool of the library — classification, cataloguing, reference service — can all by itself satisfy the varied demands of each of the readers. Only through an integrated use of the several tools can greater efficiency be achieved to the satisfaction of the Laws of Library Science. This is the right approach, the holistic approach.

CHAPTER J

LAW 5: A LIBRARY IS A GROWING ORGANISM

"Finding out what we want should become a major object of our attention . . . there is a vast difference between letting changes occur and choosing the changes we want to bring about by our technological means."

—Bertrand de Jouvenal

"Utopia for Practical Purposes"

—*Daedalus* (Summer, 1965)

1 The Human Side

In my own interpretation of Ranganathan's Five Laws of Library Science, I come full circle when I review the impact of the fifth law on my efforts and interests in librarianship. If we are to develop library service, we must effectively control the system which facilitates the interactions between reader and book. To insure proper growth we need librarians who are educated in such a way that they believe in facilitating this interaction in everything they do.

2 Professional Education

Library education for me has become the focal

point where the library profession's growth can be nurtured and guided. Libraries *are* people (both readers and literature are *not* collection of books). Library education puts me in touch with librarians who are struggling with the notion of professionalism for the first time, who are eager to learn what we know; and because they are a captive audience, I can also tell them what we do not know. Our struggles to understand ourselves and our work can be laid out before a class and they can have sport with what we know. Many of them have stimulated me to rethink the role of the librarian in society, and the place of technology in the library. These exchanges have been very exciting and I welcome every new class with open arms because I am convinced that personal growth comes through our interaction with others.

In the United States, we are engaged in a reexamination of the library profession, our work and our education, our relationship with other professionals in the information business. This creates an aura of crisis for some, but for others it has helped to clarify how we can accommodate growth, change, and new perspectives.

3 Professionalism

Several years ago, a sociologist by the name of William J Goode discussed the professional nature of librarianship. He felt that librarianship fell somewhere in the middle of a professional-nonprofessional continuum. To him, librarianship was engaged in a struggle for full professional recognition.

In this struggle, he felt librarianship had certain advantages. One, librarianship is a full-time occupation specialising in a certain area and is not subordinate to any other group, in the same status as nursing is to doctoring in medicine. Related to this is that librarians have a sense that their occupation is unique. Two, librarians are closely attached to learning which is a prime source of occupational prestige in the society. In addition, an increasing number of librarians are trained in professional schools, some of which are associated with universities and offer a doctorate. Three, librarians belong to professional associations, at local, state, and national levels. Four, librarians have formulated a code of ethics.

But Goode did feel that librarianship lacked two key attributes that keep it from becoming fully accepted as a profession. One, a prolonged specialised training in an abstract body of knowledge. Two, a collectivity or service orientation, in terms of professionally defined "needs" of its clients, rather than what its clients simply "want." I shall explain.

In terms of the knowledge base Goode maintained that librarianship had failed to develop a general body of scientific knowledge dealing with information storage and retrieval, but depended upon rather rule-of-thumb, local regulations and rules, plus a major cataloguing system for most of its day-to-day work. Even now, some librarians express doubt about the importance of formal education for librarianship. Goode maintained that the public did not believe that the librarian has a knowledge base specific to his occupation. He felt that the public views librarians as gatekeepers and custodians to a "stock room" of books and periodicals. This aspect, if true, seems to be intensified by the fact that the public largely meets only the unskilled and semi-skilled help in libraries and judges the trained librarians, who work mostly away from the eyes of the public, by the performance of the help. Even today some librarians seem to be particularly sensitive to being referred to as "gatekeepers" or some similar term. This is not to deny that others particularly seem to be proud of being called "book-keepers."

4 Library Management

According to Goode, another factor related to the knowledge base is that the librarian begins to assume administrative tasks earlier than in most other occupations. Much of this administration is not specific to librarianship, for it consists instead of integrating human beings in a corporate enterprise and not in pushing back the frontiers of knowledge in the field. Some librarians even argue that such an administrative emphasis is properly a central task of librarians. In fact, status or prestige today seems to be achieved in the field mostly by administration, that is, in taking on more administrative responsibility rather than being distinguished as a specialist.

When the administrative ladder no longer is the only way to increased status, we may be closer to calling librarianship a true profession. As the problems of handling information increase, many will have to do research similar to those I described if we are ever to cope with the fifth law. There are problems of values and changes in values of what is significant information and what is insignificant. Coping with growth may mean that we need ways of dispersing the avalanche of information so that the reader will not be overwhelmed. Efforts called S D I (Selective Dissemination of Information) come to mind very quickly. The natural extension of such efforts can be made an integral part of a library if librarians will handle *information,* not as we do today in libraries (storage and retrieval functions), but in a way that will both create and destroy it! By selecting and evaluating information, we give priorities to the contents of our storehouses. We make value commitments and we say that our choices are unbiased. Is this truly the case? Let us say that a librarian has five hundred rupees to spend. The physics department wants a reference book that costs almost the full amount. The history department wants some early works which cost about five hundred rupees. Who gets that priority? How does the librarian decide? Is history more important than physics or vice versa? If a librarian decides on some sort of comprimse, what values does he use to decide who gets what? Is a compromise a "good" thing? Why? As librarians, you know that you make similar decisions nearly every day. You decide, within certain limits, who gets what. You are faced with limits of time, finance. etc. Within the contexts of these limits, you make choices about what knowledge is to be available. You are determining the growth of the library by your decisions!

5 Growth of Knowledge

Alvin M Weinberg, who was chairman of the President's Science Advisory Committee, said that "those who control information will become a dominant priesthood in the science of the future." He is right. If our choices emphasise certain areas of science, those areas will benefit to the possible detriment of other areas. If our choices emphasise science areas, humanities areas may unduly suffer as a result. In part, our choices determine the areas of knowledge of the present and of the future. We are part of the process of knowledge creation and destruction. We should recognise this responsibility in all of our libraries and make our decisions based on more knowledge wherever possible. That is why I tried to describe some research studies in these lectures, the finding of which will affect library practice. It is a fact of life that the library is a growing organism *if* the library's staff is engaged in pursuing the other four laws. How we put our knowledge to work — the knowledge we have of ourselves and of our users — will determine our growth rate and the evaluation that society makes of the importance of our contribution.

CHAPTER K

GENESIS OF THE FIVE LAWS OF LIBRARY SCIENCE

1 Golden Jubilee of the Five Laws

Dr S R Ranganathan conceived of the Five Laws of Library Science in 1924. Four years from now, the golden jubilee of this event, which marked the transition of our discipline from "Library Economy" to "Library Science" will be celebrated. The statements embodying the Five Laws were formulated in 1928 and published for the first time in 1931 in a book of the same title (13).

It is appropriate that in an essay on the implication of the Five Laws of Library Science, we should take a brief look at the context and the causes for the formulation of the Five Laws.

2 Ranganathan's Love of Teaching

Ranganathan was appointed Librarian of the University of Madras in 1924. He was not happy to be the University Librarian. In fact he wanted to quit the post and return to his first love, namely, teaching. This was only natural. Half a century ago, library work hardly offered anything challenging, particularly to one who had a Master's Degree in

Mathematics and had already experienced the thrill and joy of teaching mathematics and physics to young, uninhibited, growing minds in the undergraduate, graduate, and post-graduate classes, for some seven years earlier. Besides, for Ranganathan, the joy was all the more because as a born teacher, he was attracted to teaching not because it offered a career, but because he had decided to make teaching his field of work. It would appear that, in spite of the desire of and pressure from, some of his elders at home wanting him to enter the lucrative civil service or the lawyer's profession, he was determined to take up teaching.

3 A Momentous Decision

Before taking a final decision to quit librarianship and return to teaching, Ranganathan listened to Mr H S Duncan, the Principal of the Presidency College, where Ranganathan had been working. He advised him against leaving the librarian's job. He said in effect, "You have not seen much of librarianship yet; you may find something in it after you have studied the subject in London; the University is deputing you shortly." Accordingly Ranganathan postponed his decision. That was a momentous decision. For, perhaps without his knowing it, a new chapter in the development of library science was begun by him at that very moment. Ranganathan was deputed to study library practices in the British Museum library in 1924.

4 Outmoded Practices and Unwanted Subjects

On his reporting himself at the British Museum Library for observation and study of library work, Sir Frederick Kenyon, the Principal Librarian, informed Ranganathan that he would be able to learn there only some eighteenth-century practices unsuitable for university library work, and that he should join the School of Librarianship, University College, London. Thanks to the sympathetic understanding on the part of the library school and of the British Museum Library authorities, Ranganathan could join the course in librarianship. There again, he found himself with the prospect of learning History of English fiction, Sanskrit grammar, German grammar, Indian palaeography, and Epigraphy, none of which would be of use to his library work in India. Thanks again to the library school authorities, he was exempted from attending the classes on these subjects.

5 Three Contextual Features

In the library school, subjects such as Classification, Cataloguing, and Reference Service attracted his attention and provided food for his thinking. He had admiration and appreciation for his teacher W C Berwick Sayers, and the latter reciprocated the same. This facilitated a good deal of intimate discussions between them on classification and other aspects of library work.

Secondly, having exempted himself from attending the courses on Sanskrit grammar, etc, Ranganathan found adequate time to read almost all the books on library work available in the libraries of the school and of the Library Association — which were not many in those days. This gave him a broad perspective and at the same time, a deeper knowledge of the library practices and library service developed and prevailing in the early twenties of the present century.

Thirdly, Ranganathan visited over a hundred libraries of different varieties — public, college, and university — in Great Britain, to observe and study library practices, first-hand.

These experiences appeared to have had a deep influence on his subsequent ideas about the library.

1 From what he saw of library service in Great Britain, he realised the great potential of the library as an agency for social advancement;

2 He made it his life's mission to secure for his motherland social progress through the promotion of library service;

3 He recognised that some empirical guiding

principles have been formulated for some aspects of library work — for example, Cutter for Cataloguing; and Richardson and Sayers for Classification. And he was already making a radical departure from the existing methodology in the design of his Colon Classification, the idea of the analytico-synthetic approach having been triggered by his observing the working of the meccano toy in Selfridge's store;

4 He recognised also that there was no unifying set of guiding principles for library practices and services as a whole; that several areas of librarianship lacked empirical principles and decisions were taken and practices devised *ad-hoc* by precedence and by trial and error. The helpfulness of the decisions depended a great deal on the flair and experience possessed by the librarian concerned; and

5 The impact of all these ideas on a man trained in systematic scientific thinking was that he intuitively saw the need for a unified theory on the basis of which every technique and practice of library service could be derived and be guided in their development.

6 The Five Laws are Born

Conceived in an incipient form in 1924 and worked upon in the following five years, the Five Laws of Library Science were formulated in the final form in 1928 and published in 1931, after being used as the basis for the teaching of every branch of library science for three years. The precipitating factor was a series of lectures that Ranganathan delivered to an audience of about a thousand teachers at the Conference of the South Indian Teachers' Union in 1928. In these lectures, he propounded his ideas on library practice and library service as derivable from the Five Laws he had then been formulating. He also showed their connection to the methods of teaching in schools and colleges.

61 First Law Emerges Last

It would appear that Ranganathan at first formulated the statement of four laws only — Law 2 to Law 5 in the present set. He felt that some vital principle was missing from the set and he was obsessed by it. At that time, his former Mathematics Professor, Edward B Ross used to visit him almost every day at the University Library. Their mutual affection was like that of brothers. Prof Ross used to discuss various library matters with Ranganathan. On one of these visits, Prof Ross sensed the anguish in Ranganathan. The latter explained what was worrying him and Prof Ross at the point of leaving the library said in effect, in a moment of intuitive flash, "you mean Books are for Use"! And so Law 1 was formulated and with it the set was complete.

62 Testing Ground

The Summer Course in library science conducted under the auspices of the Madras Library Association from 1928 and absorbed into the Madras University Department of Library Science started in 1931, was a laboratory for Ranganathan to propound his ideas in library science based on the laws and study the reaction of students. The Madras University Library was his other laboratory for testing the effectiveness of the library techniques designed by himself in terms of the reaction of readers. The blending of the findings from the two kinds of tests enabled Ranganathan, in a great measure, to formulate, elaborate, and refine most of his basic ideas on almost all facets of library service and library science with the Five Laws as the foundation.

7 Library Science and Service in a Nutshell

With the formulation of the Five Laws, a unifying theory for all library practices and services, and a set of guiding principles for the dynamic development, study and teaching of library service as a whole, became available. Postulates, canons, and principles, based on the Five Laws, for guiding the development, study, and teaching of each of the branches of library work could be derived. Changes in library practices could be predicted in the context of the changes in the needs and demands of the society; and the effectiveness of each library practice could be tested against the implications of the Five Laws. The discipline of "Library economy" completed a full cycle in the Spiral of Scientific Method and attained the status of a science (14).

To illustrate, here is a definition of the scope and content of Documentation — a modern concept — in terms of the Five Laws. Ranganathan writes (17):

"Driven by the Five Laws of Library Science and urged by the demand for nascent micro thought by specialist readers, the library profession is now faced with a new situation calling for new techniques, new attitudes, and new forms of service . . . Documentation may be defined as:

1 Promotion and practice of bringing into use of nascent micro thought by specialists (Law 1); and

2 Pinpointed (Law 2),

3 Exhaustive (Law 3),

4 Expeditious (Law 4),

service of nascent micro thought to specialists;

5 In spite of the continuous ever increasing cas-

cade (Law 5) of nascent micro thought on an ever multiplying number of subjects, communicated through several thousands of periodicals".

71 Coverage: Macro to Micro

The Laws provide guidelines not only in the formulation of a theory for large divisions of library science such as Book Selection, Classification, Cataloguing, Reference Service, Physical Bibliography, Management, Library Buildings, Fittings and Furniture, and Documentation, but they also guide Librarians to make helpful decisions on such minute aspects as "the appropriate width and treatment of the window-sill of the stack room," "the sequence of the elements in the host section of a bibliographical reference," and "the size of lettering in the shelf guides, gangway guides, and bay guides." In Ranganathan's own words, the *Five Laws of library science* "contains, in little, practically everything which is found more elaborately elucidated in all the succeeding books of the family" (15).

8 Perennial Source of Inspiration and Guidance

Elsewhere I have said: "If Dr Ranganathan had done nothing more than publish the *Five Laws of library science,* he would have to be seriously considered for a Library Hall of Fame. The impact of these five succinct statements, first published in

1931, is still being felt around the world via transmitters, namely, Dr Ranganathan's students and followers who know the importance of these laws on every continent and most every country where there is to be a philosophy of library service and development . . . The explication and amplification of these statements by teachers in library science classes also help to perpetuate his teachings because these words stir students to think of and believe in library *service* above library *work* as their life goal. Few writers have caught the essence of librarianship in such few words and have been as eloquent as Dr Ranganathan is in his several lecture tours around the world in the past forty years" (1).

Berwick Sayers, who was an important early influence on the formation of Ranganathan's early library ideas, caught the deep significance of the Five Laws in these words: "The *Five Laws of library science*, 1931 (new edition 1957), a work of great simplicity which conceals depths and yet reveals what may be called the spiritual but intensively practical springs of his activity" (20).

That the Laws are perennial sources of guidance in all library work and service is reflected in two different ways in the statements by two American teachers of library science. Talking about the func-

BIBLIOGRAPHICAL REFERENCES

Note.— 1 Col 1 gives the serial number of the Bibliographical reference.

2 Col 2 gives the section number of the text, where the reference is made.

3 Col 3 gives the bibliographical reference.

1	Sec K8	ATHERTON (P). Dr S R Ranganathan. (Library resources and technical services. 14; 1970; 582–4).
2	Sec G443	DEWEY (M). Dewey decimal classification and relative index. Ed 17. 1967. V2 (revised). N Y, Lake Placid, Forest Press.
3	Sec G42	ENCYCLOPEDIA AMERICANA. International ed. 1968. New York, American Corporation.
4	Sec G42	FERGUSON (C A). Language study and the Middle East. (Annals of the American Academy of Political and Social Science. 356; 1964; 77).
5	Sec K8	GRAVES (F H). The five laws of library science. (Special libraries. 49; 1958; 271).
6	Sec F2 F21	LIPETZ (B–A). User requirements in identifying desired works in a large library. New Haven, Yale University Library. 1970 June.
7	Sec F32	—. —. P 14–6.
8	Sec F34	—. —. P 16–20.

9 Sec E6 MACKINNON (D W). Nature of creativity. (*In* creativity and college teaching. Proceedings of a conference held at the University of Kentucky. 1963. Kentucky. College of Education, University of Kentucky, Lexington. (Bulletin of the Bureau of School Service. 35, Number 4; 1963; P 33).

10 Sec F2 PALMER (R). User requirements of a university library card catalog. 1970. (Thesis, Ph D. University of Michigan). [Unpublished].

11 Sec F21 —. —. P 66–8.

12 Sec F33 —. —. P 66–6, 73–4, 82–3.

13 Sec K1 RANGANATHAN (S R). Five laws of library science. 1931. Madras, Madras Library Association.

14 Sec K7 —. Scientific method, library science and march of digvijaya. (*In* Author's Five laws of library science. Ed 2. 1957. Chapter 8).

15 Sec K7 —. Social bibliography or physical bibliography for librarians. 1952. Delhi, Delhi University.

16 Sec K8 —. --. P 14–6.

17 Sec K7 —, *Ed*. Documentation and its facets. 1963. Sec B17. Bombay, Asia Publishing House.

18 Sec E9 RHINELANDER (P H). Education and society. (Key reporter. 1968 Autumn).

19 Sec K8 SHERA (J H). Sociological foundations of librarianship. 1970. Sec E75. Bombay, Asia Publishing House.

20 Sec K8 Sayers (W C B). Preface. (*In* Ranganathan (S R). Prolegomena to library classification. Ed 2. 1957. P 19).

21 Sec H5 Swanson (D). On improving communication among scientists. (Bulletin of atomic scientists. 1966 Feb; 10–11).

22 Sec H5 System Development Corporation. Recommendations for national document handling systems in science and technology. 1965. Appendix A, 2: 11–6).

23 Sec G42 Winchell (C T). Guide to reference books. Ed 8. 1967. Chicago. American Library Association.

24 Sec G42 Zadrozny (J T). Dictionary of social science. 1959. Washington, Public Affairs Press.

INDEX

BY MAYA BHATTACHARYYA

Note.— 1 The index number against each item is the number of the chapter and the section of its occurrence in the text.

2 The following abbreviations are used:

def = defined *qirt* = Quoted in relation to
irt = in relation to